Leveraging *the* Impact *of* Culture & Climate

DEEP,
SIGNIFICANT,
AND LASTING
CHANGE
IN CLASSROOMS
AND SCHOOLS

Steve Gruenert | Todd Whitaker

Solution Tree | Press

a division of
Solution Tree

555 North Morton Street
Bloomington, IN 47404
800.733.6786 (toll free) / 812.336.7700
FAX: 812.336.7790

email: info@SolutionTree.com
SolutionTree.com

Visit **go.SolutionTree.com/schoolimprovement** to download the free reproducibles in this book.

Printed in the United States of America

[INSERT CIP DATA]

Solution Tree
Jeffrey C. Jones, CEO
Edmund M. Ackerman, President

Solution Tree Press
President and Publisher: Douglas M. Rife
Associate Publisher: Sarah Payne-Mills
Art Director: Rian Anderson
Managing Production Editor: Kendra Slayton
Copy Chief: Jessi Finn
Senior Production Editor: Christine Hood
Content Development Specialist: Amy Rubenstein
Copy Editor: Evie Madsen
Proofreader: Kate St. Ives
Text and Cover Designer: Abigail Bowen
Editorial Assistants: Sarah Ludwig and Elijah Oates

Acknowledgments

Solution Tree Press would like to thank the following reviewers:

Michael Browne
Principal
Worcester County Public Schools
Newark, Maryland

Jennifer Evans
Principal
Burnham School, K–6
Cicero, Illinois

Alexander Fangman
Principal
Grant's Lick Elementary School
Alexandria, Kentucky

David Pillar
Assistant Director
Hoosier Hills Career Center
Bloomington, Indiana

Steven Weber
Associate Superintendent for Teaching
    and Learning
Fayetteville Public Schools
Fayetteville, Arkansas

Visit **go.SolutionTree.com/schoolimprovement** to download the free reproducibles in this book.

Table of Contents

About the Authors ix

INTRODUCTION
How Culture and Climate Can Improve Schools 1
    The Difference Between Culture and Climate 2
    Impacts of Changing the Climate to Influence Culture 4
    Theoretical Foundations of Culture and Climate 7
    About This Book 9
    Conclusion 9

CHAPTER 1
How to Define School Culture 11
    Culture Traits 12
    What Cultures Try to Do 14
    Irrational Cultures 20
    Conclusion 22

CHAPTER 2
Differences Between Culture and Climate 23
    Organizational Culture 23
    Organizational Culture Versus Organizational Climate 26
    The Confusion Between Culture and Climate Change 33
    Additional Analogies to Demonstrate the Difference
        Between Culture and Climate 38
    The Commonalities of School Culture and Climate 41
    Conclusion 41

CHAPTER 3
Elements of Climate 43
    Elements of Climate Versus Elements of Culture 43

School Climate as a Tool. 47

Conclusion 49

CHAPTER 4
Classroom Cultures. 51

The Small Culture 51

Classroom Culture as a Reflection of Teacher Attitude and Mindset 53

A Typology of Classroom Cultures 56

Classroom Culture Assessment. 66

Classroom Culture Change. 73

Conclusion 75

CHAPTER 5
The Culture Scorecard 77

Three Levels of Culture. 77

Introductions Scorecard 78

Classroom Scorecard 82

Conclusion 85

CHAPTER 6
The Capacity to Change. 87

Assumptions Guiding the Theory of Capacity to Change 88

The Process for Change 90

The Speed of Culture Change. 97

Conclusion 99

CHAPTER 7
School Culture Assessment. 101

Qualitative Research. 101

Data Analysis 105

Conclusion 105

CHAPTER 8
The Necessity of Culture Change 107

Unchangeable Cultures. 108

Warning Signs. 110

Conclusion 111

CHAPTER 9

A Closer Look at Values 113

What's Most Important in Life 114

What's Most Important at Work. 116

Value Change to Culture Change 116

Conclusion 119

CHAPTER 10

Not the Perfect Culture, the *Right* Culture 121

What the Right School Culture Looks Like. 122

Additional Thoughts for Identifying the Right School Culture 124

Conclusion 125

Epilogue. 127

Before You Begin 127

The Playbook for Culture Change 130

Conclusion 132

References and Resources 133

Index 137

About the Authors

 **Steve Gruenert** has been at Indiana State University since 2002 teaching educational leadership courses and doing research in the field of school culture and climate. He has experience as a public school teacher and an administrator at the secondary level. Steve's research into school culture started in 1996 at the University of Missouri, and he has continued to conduct research, guide dissertations, present at conferences, and write about the topic since Dr. Jerry Valentine, advisor and professor emeritus at the University of Missouri and an educational consultant, introduced it to him.

Steve has a PhD in school governance from the University of Missouri. Steve likes to play golf and fish, but he spends many hours each week thinking about the next book on school culture. This is his fourth book related to school culture and climate. Steve and his wife Emily have been married for thirty years. They have three daughters and three grandchildren.

To learn more about Steve's work, follow him @SteveGruenert on Twitter.

 **Todd Whitaker** is a professor of educational leadership at Indiana State University in Terre Haute, Indiana. One of the United States' leading authorities on employee motivation and leadership effectiveness, his message has resonated with professionals around the world. He has written more than twenty books, including *What Great Teachers Do Differently: Fourteen Things That Matter Most*; *Shifting the Monkey: The Art of Protecting Good People From Liars, Criers, and Other Slackers*; and *The Ten-Minute Inservice: Forty Quick Training Sessions That Build Teacher Effectiveness*.

Todd has a PhD in educational leadership from the University of Missouri.

To learn more about Todd's work, follow him @ToddWhitaker on Twitter, or visit www.toddwhitaker.com.

To book Steve Gruenert or Todd Whitaker for professional development, contact pd@SolutionTree.com.

INTRODUCTION

How Culture and Climate Can Improve Schools

It is amazing how you can walk into a school and immediately get a feel for what it would be like to work or learn there. Some places are inherently warm and welcoming, and others can be sterile and off-putting. Similarly, you can enter two classrooms of the same grade level or subject area and feel like you are in two different worlds. What causes this and how can the contrast be so sharp? The cultures and climates can be so dramatically different that they are overpoweringly noticeable.

We designed this book to help educators improve by understanding the impact of culture and climate on each school and every classroom. Once they can effectively look through both of these lenses—culture and climate—educators can begin to see how they are the keys to improving individual classrooms and entire schools. When you understand how culture and climate are very different and yet always conjoined, you can envision the needed steps to grow and improve your classrooms and schools. This book was written to help teachers understand the role of culture and climate in the classroom and to help school leaders—formal and informal—understand the role of culture and climate in their schools.

Soon after starting work on his doctor of philosophy degree in educational leadership, Steve's advisor handed him the book *Corporate Cultures* by Terrence E. Deal and Allan A. Kennedy (1982). This was one of the first books to draw attention to organizational culture and its importance. Using that book as a starting point, Steve expanded on the notion that organizations create their own values and belief systems, which serve as the greatest influence over employee behaviors. This isn't just a corporate phenomenon; this is something that all schools experience, and it's something all school leaders need to understand.

The Difference Between Culture and Climate

Although culture and climate are two different concepts, they clearly have strong connections. These two concepts are abstract and yet understandable. There are no clear definitions so the best way to see their interconnection is through examples. If educators do not understand the differences, it can restrict their ability to make progress and especially limit the long-term development of a desired culture. Sharing our journey may help you succeed on yours.

Culture is a complex concept. Any time a group of people spend a significant period of time together, they will develop roles and expectations for each other. Over time, these roles will define each person and give balance to the group as its members attempt to survive the environment. The group will create rules to define who is a member and who is not. Rewards and sanctions will support these rules, usually in the form of peer pressure. There is comfort and predictability as routines and rituals bond the group. Change is not welcome. A culture has been formed (Gruenert & Whitaker, 2015).

Climate is much more simplistic. Climate is a group response to a particular situation or circumstance (for example, how we are supposed to feel or the mood of the group at any given moment). This can vary quite often, such as during a faculty meeting when teachers learn there is a snow day.

We wrote this book because in all kinds of academic settings, and while reading educational publications, we find many intelligent, experienced people using the terms *culture* and *climate* interchangeably. While this may seem like a small issue, it's indicative of a much larger problem. When we find leaders thinking they can focus only on climate while not impacting the culture, or believing they can alter the culture just as easily as they can impact the climate, we know something has to change. Let's look at a couple of examples.

Imagine school *climate* as your child's body temperature. Then, imagine that his or her immune system—which is the *culture*—can influence the climate (temperature). When a virus (new culture) gets into the body, it causes a fever (climate) to emerge as a means to fight the virus. This is the immune system at work. You know the child has a fever by watching his or her behavior and using a thermometer. When there is a fever, you don't try to fix the thermometer, you try to heal the child. We often give children medicine to bring down the fever and reduce discomforts the virus brings.

While medicine might lower the fever, the virus is still there. We should not assume that a lower body temperature has rid the body of the virus, just as we should not assume that changing the climate has permanently impacted the culture. A strong virus can weaken the immune system if it hangs around for a long time. Similarly, some changes can weaken a culture in the long term as well. The child is still sick even if he or she feels better.

In this example, the virus (or change) is long term and does not disappear in a few days. However, the temperature (or climate) can move up and down or even dissipate much more quickly. Even if the fever breaks, the virus or change may remain.

To ignore the climate is to be, in the words of the legendary rock band Pink Floyd, "comfortably numb" (Gilmour & Waters, 1980). To focus completely on the climate is to be painfully aware of people's feelings, and this can potentially lead to an over-focus on climate (for example, working to make everyone happy all the time). This can lead to short-term decision making, which can prevent actual organizational growth.

A doctor usually asks his or her patient, "How do you feel?" The doctor wants the truth, but some patients still feel the need to hide it. Pain charts typically operate on a one-to-ten scale, one being minor and ten being major. Climate, like pain, can be relative. On the scale, a paper cut could be a seven for one person and a two for someone else. Typically, the culture will tell you how much pain you can show. It may reinforce complaining or discourage it. The culture can also value a positive approach, even if it is impractical.

Climate can have the same effect. If you were previously in a school that had a very positive climate, your current one may look negative in comparison and vice versa. Others in the same school may have had a previous experience that affects their perspectives. However, like the pain chart, it is true to them. For example, a new leader's assessment of the school culture might be dramatically impacted by the previous culture at his or her old school. Once you have worked with an excellent leader, you have different standards for all the leaders you will work with going forward. The previous positive experience may hurt the culture in future settings by comparison. Another challenge is if you have been in a school with a negative environment; you may actually become uncomfortable if you join a school with a more positive tone. The new setting may actually feel wrong, even if it's more positive. If your experiences are in a negative culture, you may start to feel that negative culture is what normal should look like when you move to a new site.

Some schools will champion the person who goes through the pain without complaining—suck it up and be strong. Some new teachers quickly learn that the discomfort of being new is a rite of passage, and veteran teachers may not allow any complaining, even when it is justified and potentially helpful to the long-term health of the school. There may even be an informal induction that other teachers use for new staff members. For example, established teachers may remind new staff to sit next to their most challenging students during assemblies to prevent inappropriate behavior. Conversely, veteran teachers might encourage new staff to leave the auditorium and their students unsupervised so they feel less guilty when they do this themselves.

Established staff members may coach new teachers on how frequently they should send students to the office for discipline. Typically, they will want the new teachers to stay in the "range of normal" so the veterans feel comfortable. In more effective, schools, staff listen to new teachers—the teachers who represent the future—as they have not yet assimilated into the school culture.

Impacts of Changing the Climate to Influence Culture

Using this scenario, imagine the school's culture as the immune system; the virus is a climate change. The immune system is constantly on guard and fighting off any attempts at change. When change approaches a school (for example, new policies or laws), the discomfort that comes with it can act like a fever. This can also occur if the district hires a new superintendent or there are new school board members elected who want to implement different processes. Staff will appear to be discontent, uneasy, or unhappy. They want to avoid change, tamp it down, or eradicate it. How staff feel can overpower a much-needed change. The climate of the school is a construct based on staff's feelings. If school leaders address the way teachers feel, they may try to bring down the fever, but that does not address the change—the source of the discomfort. Some school leaders may bring in food, let teachers wear jeans, or hire a motivational speaker to make staff feel better about change. Unfortunately, most actions like these that school leaders take are similar to giving a child an aspirin. The actions may have an impact, but it's at best a temporary one.

These same temporary alterations happen at the classroom level as well. If a teacher is in a good mood on Monday, his or her mood can help impact classroom climate for a day, but what he or she does on a *continual daily basis* actually determines if students come to class with a positive frame of mind or if they wait until they can establish the teacher's mood. If the teacher has a positive frame of mind every day, it can start to have an impact on classroom culture. However, if the teacher's attitude is based on which way the wind blows, if his or her team wins or loses, or the timing of next school vacation, things will always be at the climate level and the culture will depend on the teacher's changing daily climate or mood. If this continues for a long time, it becomes normal.

Most school cultures will "lie" to their members by presenting a false reality. For example, on the first day of school, everyone acts nice to each other or outwardly pretends everything is okay when it might not be. And just like the immune system is different from person to person, culture can vary widely from school to school. When the immune system, just like the culture, is unchallenged, all can seem well. But when there is a new virus (or idea), different immune systems respond in various ways—some positive and some negative. This is not inherently good or bad; it only matters whether the idea itself is good or bad. Some changes are not good and the climate changes, as the culture tries to protect the integrity of the school. For example, a revised school board policy requires a new approach to teaching reading. Some excellent veteran teachers are rightfully confident that their previous approach is better so they sneak it in whenever possible in their own classrooms.

While *culture* is a framework for solving problems, it is also the perfect mirror. If a teacher is behaving badly, it is almost a guarantee that before long, students will start behaving badly as well. When you do not like what you see in the mirror, polishing the mirror is not the solution. Even dimming the lighting may not be enough. If you want to change student behavior in the classroom, it is best to start by altering adult behavior in the classroom. Focusing on things you can change (your behavior) instead of things you can't (student behavior) will help you alter things you do not have direct influence over. For example, if a teacher would like students to behave more respectfully, the first step is for the teacher to make sure he or she always treats students with respect. A less effective teacher might emulate the students' misbehavior, thus perpetuating and reinforcing their actions. The adult has to change first.

Knowing and understanding the difference between school culture and climate will put school leaders in a better position for managing resources, goals, and outcomes. This understanding also allows principals to implement deep, significant, and lasting change in their schools. When the culture you have is the one you want, the climate will be fine. In other words, if you are a very healthy person, a slight fever does not put your overall health at great risk.

When the climate feels OK, you may not know exactly *why*. Even if you do—the weather is nice or a three-day weekend is coming—these things are uncontrollable and generally *happen to you* rather than occur *because of you*. Ironically, you may decide not to exercise because you feel good in the same way that you may avoid it when you feel bad. A teacher may allow outside things to influence the way they interact with students. If a dreary day causes a teacher to be less patient with students, they are allowing outside things or events into their classroom. School leaders can have satisfied, happy teachers in ineffective schools, especially if they survey the teachers on a sunny Friday afternoon. But if leaders have effective schools, it is much more likely that they have happy, satisfied teachers on a *consistent* basis.

Students can enter a classroom in a positive frame of mind because the football team won a big game on Friday, but that can be far from your control—even if you are the coach. This does not mean staff and students shouldn't enjoy the victory and use it to help build the underlying culture; but teachers must be mindful of how they approach students and instruction on a daily basis if they want to build an appropriate classroom climate *and* culture.

Our work with school leaders provides us with many opportunities to work with schools on a variety of challenges. We are especially interested when this work involves culture and climate. Almost everything comes from climate and culture—but this may be too reductive a viewpoint. We actually dislike using the terms *culture* and *climate* in the same sentence and hope to disentangle their close mutual association. Whether we are teaching graduate courses, consulting with schools, or supporting a statewide principal leadership initiative, we have the privilege of working with teachers and school leaders who are hoping to improve their schools. As you might expect, most conversations usually end up challenging the school culture because existing problems and issues usually have been around a long time. Typically, making improvements means changing the status quo, which is often a threat to the culture.

What tends to happen early in these conversations can at times be frustrating. Sometimes, leaders present *changing the culture* as one of many items on a list, as if it were a box to check off—similar to adjusting the lunch schedule or student pick-up and drop-off logistics. Occasionally, we might work with a school leader who announces how he or she was able to change the culture at a previous school, but it didn't last very long. Or sometimes a leader might share how he or she is now using a new program to change the culture. Moreover, some leaders use culture as an excuse for their schools' struggles or even their own ineffectiveness.

Some leaders might say, "There is nothing we can do because the culture is so negative," or "Everything is so entrenched that nothing makes a difference." This lack of efficacy can be crippling, and leaders often cite culture as an immovable cause. We cannot fault these leaders for believing as they do: chances are they heard it or read it from someone who was hoping to sell something, using the term *culture* to grab attention or provide an excuse. We shouldn't be surprised that failure follows (Sarason, 1996).

On a classroom level, the same way of thinking can limit teachers when they use family background, last years' teachers, or video games as excuses for their inability to have the student success they were hoping for. Centering on self is a much more empowering way of thinking to assist teachers in making improvements at the classroom level. Psychiatrist and author William Glasser (1994) explains in his classic book, *The Control Theory Manager*, "To be successful in life, we must evaluate ourselves and work to improve: we cannot and should not depend on others" (p. 35). To improve a school, you must understand the meaning of *culture*, the type of culture in your school, and how cultures can change (Gruenert & Whitaker, 2015). The goal should be for adults in the building, not just the leaders, to realize the choices they have and how the culture may occasionally blind them. This same thing applies to the classroom. For example, if the culture of the school encourages teachers to keep parents away because as professionals they know best, it can put pressure on teachers who would like to increase parental involvement to stop because their colleagues don't approve.

Theoretical Foundations of Culture and Climate

A quick look at some theoretical concepts may help you understand organizational climate and culture. This historical view is important, as it is the foundation of the relationships and differences between culture and climate. Relative to this conversation is what Glasser (1999) asserts with his *choice theory*. Unlike Abraham H. Maslow (1943), Glasser does not present his constructs in a hierarchy. Each need stands alone and has its own requirement to be satisfied without any influence or step approach from other needs. Glasser's (1999) *choice theory* offers five needs, including *belonging*, which is also in Maslow's (1943) hierarchy of needs. He identifies these five needs as survival, belonging, power, freedom, and fun (Glasser, 1999).

In contrast, Maslow's (1943) needs are arranged in a hierarchy, starting at the bottom: physiological and safety (basic needs), belonging and love, and esteem (psychological needs), and self-actualization (self-fulfillment needs). Basic needs must be met before psychological needs, and psychological needs must be met before self-fulfillment needs. Glasser and Maslow both recognize *the need to belong*, which represents how people are hardwired to desire connections with others. This connection usually comes with the requirement of giving up the freedom to choose all your behaviors. Typically, in an education setting, belonging needs are met by others in the school.

Sometimes, in order to fit in, we compromise our beliefs in order to belong. And usually the climate and culture tell us which path to take to fit in. Understanding the need to belong is essential to conceptualize the significance of culture in an organization. Although faculty and staff are adults, many still have part of a thirteen-year-old inside who guides their need to connect and fit in with others.

In *Critical Thinking*, the notion of *being culture-bound* describes how the beliefs of a particular group, more precisely, the *culture* of a group, can blind people who are unaware of their blindness (Paul & Elder, 2009). In other words, many behave within the norms of expected behaviors without realizing there are guardrails in place. These guardrails are often the unwritten rules we try to understand in order to belong to the group, or culture, that make us feel accepted. The longer you are in a group and the stronger the culture is, the more likely this is to occur.

There is no shortage of anecdotes and reports about successful programs that claim to change the culture of a school. Actually, we have yet to read about a program that didn't work. Just like we seldom hear about a diet concept that failed. Unfortunately, we often find when people claim they have made a culture change, they most likely have just altered the climate. If we see a blog, article, or social media post describing a culture change, it often is a misunderstanding of the term *culture*. The school may have moved in a positive direction, but it was most likely not a culture change. For example, if teachers are thirsty for change and build in new structures to support their desire to improve, this is beneficial but often will be temporary if the principal leaves; thus, it does not become embedded in the culture.

First, having teachers want change removes about 90 percent of the challenge for making school improvements. Second, increasing how much you do something simply augments a value that already exists—it does not change that value. In other words, if teachers decide to increase their use of praise, most likely praise was already valued in the school rather than a new concept that they adopted. Research points to a particular type of culture as best for schools; and this is what school leaders should try to achieve—a collaborative school culture (Gruenert & Whitaker, 2015). This type of culture does not simply allow improvement to happen—it demands it. (Deal & Peterson, 2016). The collaborative culture allows the knowledge of one to become the knowledge of all. There becomes an expectation that we work together to get better.

Culture change requires a change of values and beliefs, not just changing a few routines or rituals. There is always a significant cost—think of the pain scale—whenever there is a culture change. This is why change is difficult. If there is no pushback, nothing really changes. If the process is easy, everyone would do it. Significantly impacting climate can be quite challenging. The purpose of this book is not to discourage teachers and school leaders from addressing a culture that is supporting ineffective behaviors and practices; we do have the ability to change culture.

About This Book

Each chapter in this book can stand alone; you can start reading any chapter. Or you may choose to read the chapters in sequence and use the ideas as needed to fit your particular school.

Chapter 1 provides an overview of the traits commonly found in most school cultures. It also explains what cultures try to do in order to stay strong and keep group members involved. You can use this information as a lens to identify the culture traits in your own school. Chapter 2 defines the differences between organizational culture and climate and explains why people commonly confuse the two concepts. We offer analogies to help you understand the differences and commonalities between culture and climate. Chapter 3 focuses on the elements of climate and how they can be used as a tool to influence school improvement and culture change. Chapter 4 defines the small culture, which can exist in any school. It also offers a typology of various common classroom cultures and how to assess and identify those cultures in your school. Chapter 5 provides a culture and classroom scorecard to help you evaluate the type of culture you want at your school and in your classroom.

Chapter 6 discusses a theory to assess your school's capacity to change, along with a step-by-step process for attempting such a change. Chapter 7 reviews how qualitative research and data analysis can help you assess school culture, while chapter 8 identifies warning signs that indicate the need for culture change at any school. Chapter 9 examines one of the most important elements of culture—values. By identifying what's most important in your life and your work, you will get a clearer idea of how values influence school and classroom culture. Chapter 10 explores what the right culture looks like and some thoughts for how to identify the right culture in your school. Finally, the epilogue offers a plan for how to leverage what you have learned about culture and climate to begin the process of school change and improvement.

Conclusion

This book is not designed to condemn those who sell culture change or those school leaders who have failed to change a culture (when they espoused doing so). We know true change is difficult. Hopefully, you will obtain a greater understanding of what real culture change is, how it can happen, the role of climate, and who to avoid when the uninformed are selling their programs.

Battling against a negative climate or culture can be frustrating and exhausting. If educators do not have an understanding of what culture and climate are, and the significance they play, it may be almost impossible to have significant growth at either the classroom or school level. And although the climate and culture at the school level can be different from what they are in the classroom, understanding how to improve one helps educators understand how to positively affect the other. Let's get started!

CHAPTER 1

How to Define School Culture

Culture is a buzzword. We are bombarded with stories of how principals, coaches, and other leaders use their insight to turn around a toxic culture on a dime. Like in a game, culture offers an unwritten set of rules that tells players who to trust, who the real leaders are, when to quit, how hard to practice, and how to feel about losing a game. No wonder everyone is eager to have it. Cultures are not inherently good or bad. We would like them to be good, but that is not embedded in their nature. This book is designed to help you understand this and then provide guidance on how to improve them.

When coaches speak of *culture*, they are generally referring to watercooler talk or the informal interactions among team members when the public is not watching. What players do and talk about in the locker room influences much of their behavior in a game. What happens in the locker room may affect things outside the locker room, but team rules and coaches forbid players from disclosing specific details. These details might be the secret to success. Other players and coaches will soon ostracize those who choose to share those secrets. Similarly, the way teachers interact in the hallways, lunchroom, workroom, or parking lot impact how they perform in their classrooms. These informal areas in and around the school building could be teachers' "locker rooms."

The value of informal leaders for any team and how they choose to approach the game greatly influences the rest of the team. A negative player on the team impacts the locker room. You can have an all-star on the team, but if this player is constantly complaining, whining, or demonstrating a poor work ethic, it gives unspoken permission—or even an expectation—for everyone else to act the same way if the leaders do nothing. This also can happen in the workrooms, lunchrooms, or at the copy machine of any school or organization.

Culture traits are sometimes identified with certain buzzwords familiar in education settings. But culture is defined by more than its traits.

Culture Traits

The word *culture* has become vogue regarding anything that claims to influence how well a school performs or as a marketing tool for selling the latest innovation. While many new innovations may actually help improve a school, rarely will anything change the culture—educators want culture to be difficult to change. Inherently, one of the cores of any culture is that it never wants to change and it doesn't even want individuals to be outside the circle of what it considers normal. Some leaders might want to hijack a school culture as a concept to get peoples' attention. This can best be demonstrated when people claim they are going to build (or have) a culture of _____. Here is a list of school traits that one might find salespeople trying to market as the next culture of _____. Sometimes people do this to draw attention to themselves and their settings, and sometimes they do this because they do not understand the depth of organizational culture.

- *Nonviolence*
- *Kindness*
- *Critical thinking*
- *Honesty*
- *Gratitude*
- *Trust*
- *Growth mindsets*
- *Friendliness*
- *Happiness*
- *Humor*
- *Intelligence*

- *Good will*
- *Optimism*
- *Hope*
- *Positivity*
- *Efficacy*
- *Caring*
- *Collaboration*
- *Urgency*
- *Lifelong learning*
- *Empathy*
- *Morality*

- *Self-discipline*
- *Pride*
- *Efficacy*
- *Humility*
- *Respect*
- *Resilience*
- *Integrity*
- *Creativity*
- *Responsibility*
- *Courage*

The problem with this type of declaration is that the leader has decided to adopt a new trait and express it as culture. This trait, say *courage*, becomes the focus. Courage does not define the whole culture, nor does it shift the culture in a different direction. Courage was always there as a value; the school just decides to let it shine brighter for a while. Thus, it is not a culture *of* courage, it is the same culture, with *a focus on* courage.

Chances are that your school already demonstrates all the traits from the previous list to some degree. And over time, the culture may have drifted away from some traits and elevated others. This usually indicates an unneeded culture change; you already value these traits, but you need to put more energy into them. Therefore, the trait becomes a new focus for a period of time as "the flavor of the month." To elevate the trait of *caring*, for example, you know you already care to some degree, you just want to care *more*. This is not a culture change. This could be a climate alteration, and it eventually could become a more important part of the culture, but only after a significant length of time being embedded into daily practice in the school.

For example, in order for there to be a *culture change focused on caring*, caring has to become the most important thing the school embraces, celebrates, passes on to new people, and protects. It takes a great effort to make everyone aware of how valuable caring is to the school. There is nothing wrong with adopting a more caring school, or any of the traits previously listed, and increasing the degree to which the school wishes to emphasize how much it values a trait. The problem arises when a school decides to adopt one trait each year, or a few traits each year, as if the "trait of the year" can move or change a culture.

For a school to actually build a new trait at the level of culture, such as *building a collaborative school culture*, the school needs to invest time and resources into this effort. The time and effort needed comes from something else, something the school must decide—intentionally or not—that has become less important. For someone to become an expert in something, research tells us it takes ten thousand hours of deliberate practice (Gladwell, 2013). This is ten hours per week for ten years. Imagine anyone attempting to be world class at more than one endeavor, such as a world-class violinist and a world-class weightlifter. Devotion to two aspirations will cost something. Often, you hear of how world-class athletes' training can create struggles in other parts of their lives due to their commitment to becoming something special. A change in the culture demands this level of commitment (Gruenert & Whitaker, 2019).

A strong culture should not need promotion. No one should feel the need to state aloud that their culture is one of caring; it should be obvious if caring exists in the culture. If the leader claims the organization will build a caring culture, you might assume; the culture was not previously caring enough, staff have the capacity to change and become stronger at caring, and there is sufficient buy-in to sustain the effort. When the effort to change is not really at the culture level, people begin to realize the depth of commitment needed to make a real culture change, which may hinder future attempts.

Would it be better to think of a caring *climate* rather than culture? A caring climate is much easier to see and, over time, can become more embedded into the culture. Doing something every day creates a natural evolution of change. This is typically what leaders mean when they claim to change the culture; they really want to change the climate. To sustain climate changes, critical parts of the culture need to support these changes. Over time, the whole culture can support this new climate if the school leaders can sell it.

For example, the culture needs to support teachers going to extracurricular activities to show support for their students outside the classroom. The culture may try to inhibit a teacher doing so if the union frowns upon these kinds of actions or informal pressure comes from colleagues to not go above and beyond required conduct (for example, working beyond regular school hours). However, if the culture supports teachers reaching out in this way, then this would be okay or even encouraged informally.

To say something is part of your culture is giving it the highest score, the highest impact, and the largest magnitude of influence possible. Nothing is stronger than saying "it is part of the culture." To casually claim something as part of the culture, when it has moderate impact on what you do, is to discount your own understanding of the concept. Part of understanding culture is knowing what it actually does or tries to do.

What Cultures Try to Do

Where do cultures come from? What is their purpose? These two questions have driven entire bodies of research and thinking, and were one of many incentives for us to write this book. Even so, a more poignant question has emerged for understanding how cultures work: What are cultures trying to do? Knowing the answer to this might *reveal more rules of the game*—meaning that you can play the game better once you understand it. The example of extracurricular activities attendance can increase or decrease depending on the unwritten rules among school faculty. First, we will look at what cultures do in general before trying to determine what your own culture is trying to do.

Following are a few things cultures can do.

- **Minimize diversity of thought:** Typically, we do not want to minimize diversity of thought. Culture wants everyone to think and act the same. Although this is not a positive, it is what cultures do. They want people and approaches to stay constant and be alike. Oliver Sibony (2020), a professor, writer, and keynote speaker, writes that *diversity of experiences* provides a better team than diversity of appearances. Cultures aim and desire to get everyone on the same page, valuing the same values. The current culture can view diversity as a threat if people do not assimilate soon. Those who toe the line will be rewarded; members will ostracize those who do not. While this might automatically seem like a bad thing, it is what cultures do, and it is how groups survive. Think about developing a vision for the organization: at some point, you will need a convergence of opinions as to the best vision statement. This convergence represents minimizing diversity of thought. People need to be on the same page about the vision of their school.

- **Assimilate opinions:** Similar to diversity of thought, culture takes it a step further and demands that you not only value what the group values, but also publicly espouse these values (Schein, 1985; Whitaker, 2020). In other words, know the "company line" and be ready to express it when given the opportunity. Administrators, teachers, and all other staff are seen and heard throughout the community, and community members often ask them about the school. The culture is the personality of the school and thus, it becomes easier to understand. Think of it as having human traits, flaws, and strengths. The culture wants people to tell the same stories about the school. Even if staff are not completely honest about the school, the culture wants everyone to share the same inaccurate stories. We can make people out to be heroes or villains. We can share that a former teacher was rude to the principal and describe it as good or bad. This story helps people understand what behavior is valued in the school. When you take a new position, look at the people who have been there a long time. Chances are, you will become like them, not the other way around (Barker, 2017).

- **Teach survival skills:** The basic purpose of a culture is to teach the next generation how to survive and thrive using wisdom from the previous generation. In schools, new teachers quickly learn the rules—both written and unwritten—of how to survive their first year at this school, or they can have a culture that wants new teachers to be celebrated and understand the rewards of being a teacher. Whether fresh out of college or moving from another school, members of the culture will ask newbies to praise the current system or leave. This is true whether the current system is right or wrong. The culture wants to maintain status quo, so it doesn't want anyone stepping outside of the established boundaries. People can either join the club (culture) or leave and find a new club (school). It would be rare for any new staff to criticize what veteran teachers do. If, however, a new teacher arrives with messages that resonate with some respected veteran teachers—perhaps having knowledge of new systems the state is adopting—the culture may allow some changes. Keep in mind that the culture is represented by what people tell others to do or not to do through their words and actions. When we use the word *culture*, we also mean the people who are in that culture. A culture is not only something we have, but it can be something we are.

- **Attract or repel others:** It's important to be able to identify who is on the team and who is not, and who you can trust to have your back. This is important to all members of the school as well as leaders. In most organizations, there are some people who always want to help and others whose main goal is to help themselves. They may both outwardly be friendly, but their aims can be different. The culture provides opportunities for members to show people which side they are on and close the door on all others. For example, a new teacher may feel pressure to laugh at jokes that aren't really appropriate simply to fit in or avoid the judgement of others. They may be hesitant to stand up for something that is right or against something that is wrong. When we watch others attempt to stand up against the norm, the results of this effort can strengthen or even weaken our resolve to go against the cultural norms in a school. To argue that a culture is inviting to all people and all ideas is actually to say there is no culture.

- **Identify opponents:** This is a sensitive aspect of what cultures do because for a team to bond, it needs to set goals before identifying what or who might keep members from reaching those goals. Most often there will be faces or names that come with that list of problems a team may face as it addresses its goals; these are the team's opponents. These are neither good nor bad; they are just individuals who are opposing the current culture regardless of whether they are working to move it in a positive or negative direction. How much time do coaches spend studying their opponents and using their opponents as motivation?

- **Identify leaders:** Sometimes leaders are not the ones with titles. The leaders hold the values and beliefs of the culture so deeply that they earn influence over others. Others will typically let those who glorify "the way we do things around here" speak the most. Those who do this with loud voices are typically considered cultural leaders.

- **Identify who to trust and who to listen to:** As previously noted, there will be people who you can and cannot trust both inside and outside the organization. For example, a culture can "tell" its members to trust police, regardless of whether or not the police are members of the organizational culture. Cultures are built with stories, and cultural leaders allow only certain people in the culture to *own* those stories. All other members can tell the stories, but cultural guards only give a few the permission to serve as keepers of these stories. They may not be the leaders of the culture, but educators usually call on them when they need the history of the organization to prove something does or does not work there.

- **Build psychological comfort through patterns:** People love patterns. Cultures create conditions so people can pretty much run on default mode most of the day—no thinking required. People may create or perpetuate cultures that let them develop work patterns that don't require them to think. For example, if school norms are very tightly held, then the staff have little need to make decisions, as these decisions are determined for them by the culture; "group think" comes to mind. The more people simply go through the motions of each day, the stronger the culture becomes. Decisions become no-brainers, and *just use common sense* becomes the mantra. Most situations have preset reactions for members to follow, such as when to send a student to the office, where to park cars in the morning, or where to eat lunch. The fewer decisions we make during the day, the better our day might be.

- **Reward loyalty:** You might typically think of rewards as money or other tangible items to use as motivators or incentives to get people to behave properly. The culture uses information, psychological comforts, and collegiality as rewards for those who conform. The culture—or the people who maintain it—may choose to make people feel unwelcomed by not sitting by them or snubbing their invitation to Friday happy hour. Conversely, they may welcome others actions by including them the next time. At the end of the day, these three aspects of organizational work may be the most important for those who choose to stay. These can matter more than how much teachers get paid.

- **Hide:** Yes, cultures hide, which makes them stronger. Cultures can prevent you from understanding culture (Barker, 2017). Staff who have worked in a school for a period of time begin to think whatever happens around here, good or bad, is normal. Thus, the culture is able to be invisible to school staff as it promotes itself.

- **Convince members that what they tend to do is normal, and normal is good:** If most teachers are harsh disciplinarians, it might begin to feel odd if you are not the same. Teachers who do not want to treat their students like this will begin to camouflage their behavior by closing the classroom door. The opposite is also true. Teachers who choose to fit in will parade their efforts, making their classroom behaviors obvious to others. Both groups are doing this so they can fit into the culture and feel as though they belong.

Given this list, we are compelled to share the things that cultures *do not* do, whether we want them to or not.

- **Make you happy:** Culture simply defines *happiness* and creates conditions for it to exist. Many stories remove information (Barker, 2017). For example, if everyone criticizes the principal, but you like her, you have to hide your feelings or risk rejection from the majority group. As long as the story is believable and makes others feel good, people will overlook inaccuracies.

- **Improve test scores:** You can improve the culture while never seeing a change in test scores and vice versa.

- **Hire good people:** The culture can attract good or bad people, but it does not do the hiring itself.

- **Glorify the unknown:** While this may sound strange, culture gets credibility from what you know works, usually from past successes. The culture will not value an unknown future unless it sufficiently reflects past behaviors. For example, if everyone laughs at a someone's jokes, we notice and also might laugh, even if we don't think the jokes are funny. Thus, we may begin to value things we do not have much knowledge about, just to fit in, but the culture will not value the unknown practices, people, or systems.

Now that you know what culture is, where it comes from, and what it does and doesn't do, let's examine school culture through a different lens. See figure 1.1 to determine how these culture *traits* look at your school.

What Culture Does	What This Looks Like at Our School	Is this positive or negative?
Minimize diversity of thought		
Assimilate opinions		
Teach survival skills		
Attract or repel others		
Identify opponents		
Identify leaders		
Identify who to trust and who to listen to		
Build psychological comfort through patterns		
Reward loyalty		
Hide		
Convince members that what they tend to do is normal, and normal is good		

Figure 1.1: What is your school culture doing?

*Visit **go.SolutionTree.com/schoolimprovement** for a free reproducible version of this figure.*

Review figure 1.1 (page 19). If your school culture is doing positive things, then leave it alone. However, if what your culture is doing creates a negative culture, how should you behave differently in order to have a more positive outcome? The first trait of any culture is to minimize diversity of thought. Does this mean closing down people before they have a chance to speak? Or could it manifest as a consensus among stakeholders from various communities, after everyone has aired their concerns after serious discussions?

Another thing cultures do is teach survival skills. For example, if you consistently stay late after school or come in extra early, and a few veteran staff members disapprove because they don't want to feel the pressure to do the same, you might keep your classroom door closed before or after school. In a negative culture, you might find the veteran teachers ganging up on new teachers, using a form of hazing to threaten the newbies with social isolation if they do not comply. In a positive culture, we might find principals asking the best teachers to meet with new teachers throughout the first year, asking about the challenges they are facing and perhaps learning from the new teachers what might need to change in the culture.

Most educators want to fit in and be part of the culture in which they live and work. The culture may be especially confusing when educators are in a new school or situation, and everyone else seems to know the unwritten rules and expectations. Although it's very common, the ritual of conformity might be considered irrational to those seeking improvement.

Irrational Cultures

For the purposes of this chapter, we're using the term *rational* to mean an approach to life based on logic, absent the influence of emotion. The term *irrational* would mean making decisions based purely on emotion or ignoring objective data. When things make sense or are rational, they are easy to understand. However, it's much more difficult to understand irrational cultures. Thus the purpose of this section is to try to make sense of what doesn't make sense—irrational cultures.

Cultures are invisible shelters people build for surviving the environment; cultures are the hardwiring humans have that bring them together into groups, building a sense of unity (or tribalism) as they face various threats, such as acquiring food, shelter from weather, or not being accepted, feeling lonely, and so on. People join groups so they can develop relationships and feel safer when threats do appear. Trust emanates from emotions and feelings much or more than it does from objective thinking. At times, we have to trust strangers or give people who have hurt us a second chance.

Both of these things are irrational on the surface. Trust is what turns a group into a team, tribe, or cult. It makes sense to join a tribe when the environment is threatening. When the environment is conducive to easy living, there is little need to ask others for help. People need relationships the most when things get tough. They need culture all the time, but only realize the magnitude of what it does when it is missing.

In effective schools, leaders rarely ask teachers to confront problems alone. In ineffective schools, leaders might force new teachers into challenging situations with no help. All new teachers should have the opportunity to become great educators; however, in some schools, the toxic culture will not allow that to happen.

We study school cultures because of the impact they have on adult behaviors. The optimal school culture is the collaborative school culture (Gruenert & Whitaker, 2015). One obvious tenet of this approach to problem solving—cultures are, at their best, frameworks for solving problems—is that a group can usually do a better job than an individual, especially when an individual is struggling. In other words, when a school culture is positive and collaborative, the staff want to help others become successful. This is a very desirable culture.

Typically, when small groups come together to accomplish tasks, leaders expect relationships to form, especially if the task is critical or could last a long time before completion. This bonding builds interdependence as group members determine roles. These roles may even come with assigned scripts. If you are the class clown (as an adult or student), you have to be funny. If you are the leader (formal or not), you are expected to lead. Loyalty to the group could eventually influence a member's decision making in areas that extend beyond the jurisdiction of the original charge. In other words, friendships may create loyalties to others (for example, cliques) that could outweigh the mission of the school or district. The peer pressure to do things you may not have done alone becomes a real force. Often, you become friends with others, and often those relationships endure should you move to another town or school.

This is the irrational piece: educators join groups to do a better job, yet the power of the group can sway them to compromise effective behaviors, perhaps to the point of behaving irrationally as means for protecting their membership in the group. The group may decide to go out for drinks after a long session at work, decide to come in early on a Saturday to work, or begin to adopt competitive behaviors that pit the group against other subgroups (for example, different grade-level teams) in the school. None of these behaviors are choices group members would make alone, but to continue working with this group, members now have to conform to some behaviors they would rather not do. If the group is highly successful, leaving is more difficult. It becomes rational to stay.

Whether we join extracurricular groups or our colleagues for dinner, whether we go to the basketball game on Friday, or how often we wear jeans to work are all examples of potentially altering our natural wish to fit in to the group or culture. Some groups might reward acting foolish, and soon the foolishness fades away and the behaviors become part of who they are.

Conclusion

To change a culture is to take on the biggest challenge in any school or organization. And the culture we might most want to change and have the most difficulty doing so is the irrational culture. It's hard to make sense out of something that makes no sense. What most schools probably mean to do is not so much adding something new to an existing culture as much as reintroducing something that was once there.

Changing a culture should be about rebuilding things such as interpersonal chemistry, how relationships matter, trust, patience, and capacity to change. Building trust may be the most important reason for any type of school-improvement initiative, as trust far outweighs money as an incentive (Glasser, 1994; McGregor, 1960). Changing a culture could be about restoring balance to an informal social structure. There's a reason people first created this organization. Find those reasons and tell those stories, because that is the part of a stronger culture waiting to return to work.

There is a reason we became teachers—to have a positive impact on others. If we can get back to those original reasons we became teachers—for example, the excitement of the first-year teacher—it can help us move the culture in a positive direction.

You can use culture to your advantage rather than trying to stifle it. Let culture do its thing in a way that is beneficial and positive. If we have a negative culture, doing nothing guarantees negative things will happen. If there is a good and positive culture already in place, we want to work to nurture and maintain the positive components.

CHAPTER 2

Differences Between Culture and Climate

This chapter will help refine what culture and climate *are* and what they *are not*. Through everyday examples, we show how people are members of many different cultures, including at home, at work, and in the community. Once they are involved in these cultures, the culture and climate can become almost invisible to members. What may have seemed unique on someone's first day teaching or in a new job can become routine much more quickly than you might imagine. Others' behaviors no longer seem unusual and can easily influence your own expected behaviors. Becoming more aware of this trend enables you to understand why it can be difficult to alter a culture; everyone in the culture sees the behaviors as normal, or common sense. Starting with this understanding allows you to learn how to change those things that need to change and embrace what is working well.

The stories educators tell in school can often help them more clearly see what the culture values. Who are the heroes and the legends? What did past leaders do that educators celebrate or criticize? When educators can change the stories, they can change the culture. In this chapter, we offer descriptive stories to help build understanding of this concept.

Organizational Culture

Review the description of culture in the introduction (page 1). However, another way of understanding organizational culture is to consider what it is *not*. It has little to do with each member's religion, ethnicity, race, gender, sexual orientation, or *cultural competence* (the ability to understand, appreciate and interact with people from cultures or belief systems different from one's own; DeAngelis, 2015). Organizational culture is a local phenomenon that occurs when a group of people spend significant time together. They may be close physically or even virtually—whatever environment facilitates the development of a group-based mentality. Each individual member conglomerates his or her values together with others' values and all members mold them to form a new, teamwide ideology that can be difficult to break through.

Even when it comes to something as rigid as religion, different churches in the same denomination can have very different practices. While this may depend on the leadership within individual congregations, influential members, unwritten rules, and social cliques often affect practices—all of which can last far beyond an individual leader.

Now, let's revisit the past to learn how culture and climate became so central to school effectiveness. Looking through educational leadership textbooks from decades past, the topic of culture seems to become more popular with each passing year. In the 1960s, *culture* might have received a paragraph in a book—then coined as *ethos*—while now you find whole chapters and even numerous books dedicated to culture. Many books have been published on organizational culture, most of which come from the business and management fields (see anything by former Massachusetts Institute of Technology management professor Edgar H. Schein, starting in 1985). Businesses, organizations, and sports teams all regularly note the impact of culture on their successes or lack thereof. The term *culture* has become quite vogue in 2021.

The world of education validated the concept of culture as a major factor when school effectiveness and school improvement became hot topics in the late 1970s, with works from former Yale University psychology professor emeritus Seymour B. Sarason (1971) and former University of Chicago education professor Dan C. Lortie (1975). The literature began to discriminate between effective cultures and ineffective cultures with writings from University of California Berkeley education policy professor Judith Warren Little (1990), author Susan J. Rosenholtz (1991), and education reform authority Michael Fullan (1997). Then in 1999, coauthors Terrence E. Deal and Kent D. Peterson (1999) provided one of the best books on school culture and how it works (*Shaping School Culture: The Heart of Leadership*).

In chapter 1 (page 11), we provide a quick look at how the topic of school culture has gained the attention of marketers. It seems that once *culture* became a buzzword in education, many publishers were quick to encourage writers to get the topic into their books, if not just the titles of the books, regardless of what the book was about. And, unfortunately, much of what educators read still doesn't accurately explain how culture and climate differ. Rather than providing a critique of these works, we want to help broaden the understanding and application of culture and climate related to schools and classrooms.

School cultures evolve over time. This becomes a social architecture that not only provides educators with stability and comfort but also induces limitations and restrictions on them. As more staff members buy into a dominating belief system, the culture becomes stronger and thus more resistant to change. Clearly, if everyone agrees with something it will be more difficult to alter than if there is not a consensus. Keep in mind that this is not inherently good or bad; it's just true.

Routines and traditions canonize the values that undergird the culture. Members tend to behave in ways that align with the cultural norms. Behaviors that might have initially seemed strange to a new teacher become normal over time and "hide" safely in the norms. For example, if teachers grade papers at faculty meetings, the first time one sees this, it might seem rude and unprofessional. However, eventually other teachers start to expect it and at some point may join in. Routines that may feel strange at first eventually only feel strange when members alter or break them. An unwritten framework of building-level norms and expectations will command teacher behavior more than any leader, handbook, or policy. The more invisible an organization's culture, the more influence these norms and expectations have.

For example, it may seem strange when you go to a new church that everyone sits in the same seats each week. But if you think that is strange, just wait until someone sits in one of the regular's spots. If you are new to the church, it might seem unusual. However, once others indoctrinate you into the culture it only seems unusual if patrons don't follow the unwritten seating chart. This same thing often occurs in school. Are there emotionally reserved parking places in the faculty lot? Do teachers have an expectation for where they sit in the teachers' lounge or at staff meetings? Even if there is no seating chart, how often do students return to their same seats in the classroom?

Consider a situation in which someone tells an unusual or even inappropriate joke or story in a group. New group members look around to see if others are laughing, embarrassed, or uncomfortable. If they are, the new members see the person who told the tale as the outsider. If the others do not react like they were shocked or offended, new group members might see the storyteller as the leader. Already, the others have adjusted the new members' morality scale. In any classroom at the start of the year, when a student behaves inappropriately, the students look to see how the teacher responds or doesn't respond. This starts to determine the norms (culture) in the classroom. Students are just as likely to join the crowd as adults are.

The COVID-19 pandemic provides many poignant examples of this, the most obvious being wearing masks. Todd works out at the same gym every day. When it reopened during the pandemic, some people wore masks and others did not. He noticed two very big weightlifters working out together, not wearing masks, and mocking mask wearers in their conversation. The next day, one of them was in the gym with a different partner. This new partner put on his mask, and the person who was there the day before exclaimed, "I forgot my mask in the car; I'll be right back!" Peer pressure? Sure, but multiply that to include entire teams of teachers and staff members, and it becomes an entirely different situation.

Organizational Culture Versus Organizational Climate

Though *versus* is really not the best way to look at it, taking this viewpoint may assist with the understanding of both concepts as well as help clarify their connectivity. *Organizational culture* is different from *organizational climate* (Gruenert, 2008). This idea may be the most difficult concept to get into people's schema of organizational behavior. Culture is more like a religion that guides peoples' behaviors, while climate is simply the attitudes that are acceptable given certain situations. For instance, an example of climate is when a teacher questions a superintendent's decision he disagrees with. An example of culture is when the teacher disagrees with the superintendent's decision before he even knows what the decision is. Cultures give permission for climates to behave as they do. For example, cultures tell the climate to be less perky on Monday than on Friday. For example, people may be happier on Fridays because the culture supports that. And members of a culture may not only support people being negative about Mondays they may also accept and expect them to be.

Compare how a family acts at home when they are together and how they may behave differently when they have company. And the behavior can change depending on who the company is. After a while, everyone knows the routine and immediately goes into different behaviors that reflect the norm when it is just the family. Interestingly, outsiders can also have an impact. For some guests, they clean the house top to bottom, while others get no such special treatment.

Todd's son ran cross-country and often brought his teammates home after the races. Every weekend, the team congregated at his home. Todd's family did not take their shoes off when they entered the house. When the cross-country team started coming over, the first boy who arrived asked if he should take off his shoes when he came into the house. The family told him it didn't matter to them, but he did it anyway. All twenty kids took off their shoes every time—even Todd. What is interesting is that Todd still takes off his shoes when he enters the house, even though his son's cross-country days are well behind him.

The assumptions members hold are the most definitive and yet elusive footprints of any culture (Schein, 2017). Footprints are the imprints a culture leaves behind even though we may not have seen it walk through the room. Assumptions come from values and beliefs. Values and beliefs affect what senses perceive; if you don't believe it, you won't see it (see The Ladder of Inference referred to in Senge, Kleiner, Roberts, Rosse, & Smith, 2014). The *Ladder of Inference* claims that our experiences enable or even cause us to make shortcuts, ignoring some information. Prejudices and biases are common examples. In other words, people "select the stimulation that [they] wish to perceive, based on [their] expectations, [their] needs, and [their] wants. . . . Nothing is easier than corroborating [their] own prejudices" (Robbins & Finley, 2000, p. 168). In schools, educators must be aware of what they believe about learning and teaching, and consider how those beliefs influence their decisions and practices. Simply put, administrators and teachers must be aware of their assumptions. This is the deepest level of culture (Schein, 2017).

Another reason that it can be difficult to alter a group belief is the concept of *confirmatory bias* (Sibony, 2020). This is when people create a bubble by surrounding themselves with people who believe what they believe, and they search out information that supports what they believe. Politics is an easy example. Blaming society for a teacher's ineffectiveness is another. Television stations, websites, and social media feeds can confirm any thought, belief, or even conspiracy theory a person has. This not only allows something negative to continue but also actually provides an endless stream of validation as well—whether the thought, belief, or conspiracy theory is true or not. The culture in a school can serve this purpose as well. Small groups within a culture—*subcultures*—can also create and support differing views within the same school or organization. A grade level at an elementary school and a department at a high school are common examples. Others could be coaches, or sponsors of clubs.

For school leaders to discriminate between the constructs of school culture and school climate, in the following two sections, we provide a series of scenarios that introduce the kinds of realistic situations school leaders may face. The first section provides scenarios related to culture, not climate, while the second section provides scenarios more related to climate, not culture.

Culture, Not Climate

Let's take a look at some scenarios that provide some clarification between culture and climate. The following issues speak to the culture of a school, not the climate. See if you can think of similar situations in your own education setting. Think about why you believe it is important to distinguish the differences between culture and climate.

CULTURE SCENARIO ONE
Response to Changing Student Demographics

At Hillside Elementary School, the demographics of the student population have been changing; the student population is different from those that historically attended Hillside and that teachers have grown accustomed to and comfortable with. The general response from teachers has been to keep teaching as they have always taught, waiting for new students to adapt. Over the years, school leaders have hired some new teachers, hoping a new mindset might take over because there seems to be a high degree of cynicism among the veteran faculty. Unfortunately, most of the new teachers soon adopted the practices of the veteran teachers, who refused to change. A few veteran teachers have attempted to create more inclusive classrooms only to be chastised by the other teachers.

In this scenario, a few veteran teachers are indoctrinating the new teachers, ensuring that a more effective change never takes hold. In this school, you might find a strong culture that has become resistant to change, even though teacher satisfaction levels may be high. The climate of this school does not give you a clue that there might be dysfunction (negativity, cynicism or hopelessness) in the faculty.

The culture of this school is one that allows—or demands—new teachers listen to veteran teachers if the new teachers want the support of their coworkers. A principal seeking to change the school's culture and coming into this situation would be challenged to find ways to get new teachers early in their first year away from veteran teachers who are resistant to change.

What often happens in this situation is the more innovative teachers learn to keep such innovation a secret so they do not incite the wrath of their colleagues. Although some teachers implement highly innovative practices, they are invisible to others who might want to try out new concepts. The culture encourages silence. This same thing can happen in a successful school with a few people who are using ineffective approaches. They keep their approaches under wraps and thus, their subculture group does not grow either. In a culture in which teachers are fragmented and isolated, the weakest link does not impact the whole chain.

CULTURE SCENARIO TWO
The School Is Always Right

At Pearson Middle School, the teachers have great reputations in the community. The community trusts what the teachers do and have very little reason to interfere with their work. The principal has been there a long time and has also gained the community's confidence. All teachers seem happy and love coming to work, and it shows whenever someone performs a climate audit. The trust is so embedded that if a parent ever does have an issue, he or she is too embarrassed to bring it up. For example, if a parent feels the homework is too burdensome or student discipline seems harsh, the school is always right. The school allows parents to visit during open house, fundraisers, and fairs, yet it's understood that they are not supposed to interrupt classes during school hours; they cannot challenge the weak teachers; and they cannot criticize the administration. The school seems to be a happy family, but to some, it is a sleeping dog.

In this school, the faculty have strong levels of satisfaction, loyalty, and morale. The culture (and established faculty who represent it) will challenge a new principal who allows a critical voice from the community into the school. For the school to improve with a new leader, teachers will need to relearn how to listen, and parents will need to relearn how to speak. Both teachers and parents will see this as an uncomfortable change. School leaders must build structures and events for parents and the community to have a greater influence in the daily operations of the school without the staff viewing them as threats to the peace.

CULTURE SCENARIO THREE
It's All About Football

Washington High School is a powerhouse every year when it comes to state high school football rankings. The coach has been there for twenty years, working with some of his players since they were in third-grade peewee football. The coach has a reputation as being loud and taking up a lot of space

continued ⇨

whenever he is in a group of people. Given his success over the years, he has been able to check out of a few meetings that administrators require all other teachers to attend. Lately, he has been able to get his assistant coaches out of these meetings too.

The faculty has grown used to this special treatment, and most even like it because his arrogance never seems to make a positive contribution to the meetings. When he is out of the building, the climate of the school, faculty meetings, and hallway discussions are better. The rest of the faculty have come to appreciate and expect him to be out on the football field all day and seem to benefit from his lack of collaboration with other faculty.

Again, the climate of the school is unable to reveal a problem with the culture. The administration has found a way to reward negative behavior, and the culture has become a safe place for an ineffective faculty member to thrive. A new principal inheriting this situation would be wise not to try and change it quickly. The new principal might ask the coach to attend a few meetings to give him the opportunity to share successes on the football field and listen to successes his players may be having in school. From his vantage point, the coach might begin to welcome conversations about players who may be less than successful academically or behaviorally, perhaps listening to other ideas or offering his own.

One of the difficult things to change about this situation is that all the assistant coaches, new and veteran alike, now expect that they are not part of the faculty and thus, do not have to follow the school rules and norms. If one of the assistants eventually replaces the existing coach, he or she will think it is normal not to participate. If the school hires an outsider as coach, the administrators will have to alter the mindset of the existing assistants because they have been groomed not to expect to participate.

Now we will discuss climate-driven situations. It's important to remember that things happening with the climate can sometimes be a result of the culture, making it difficult to fully separate the two.

Climate, Not Culture

The following scenarios speak to the climate of a school, not culture. The climate determines how we react to temporary changes in a school, such as treats at a faculty meeting, a fire drill, or an unexpected early dismissal. They come and go as the situation varies. See if you can think of similar situations in your own educational setting.

CLIMATE SCENARIO ONE
Students Without Pencils

Nothing is more frustrating to some teachers than students who come to class unprepared. It's as if they believe students actually have pencils but refuse to bring them just to see how upset their teachers will become. At Seaside Elementary School, one such teacher gets frustrated by this daily.

Being prepared for class is important, but lacking preparation should not interfere with the learning objectives. Teachers who ask students to use pencils should have a box of pencils ready for students to borrow. This teacher should get on with class and not make it a ritual to punish students who are missing pencils. This one teacher may bring down the morale of a whole group of teachers due to one student not being in compliance by incessantly complaining about it and griping about a lack of discipline or support from the principal.

This teacher shares her troubles too much. This is a climate issue. There is no need to assume there is a problem with the culture. The principal may choose to visit with this teacher to address individual inappropriate behaviors. If these behaviors continue, go unaddressed, or become commonplace among other teachers, it may start to affect the culture.

If this teacher continues to complain to other teachers in an unbridled fashion, the culture may determine whether or not a negative clique grows around this issue. If the culture is not a negative one, other teachers may rebuke or at least ignore the griper. If the school culture is negative, this one teacher may remind everyone else that it is time to complain. New teachers are looking for direction. If the negative voices are the only ones they hear, these newbies may feel obligated to try using negative language themselves because they want to fit in. If the leader is able to objectively monitor the trends—for example, if this negative group is getting bigger or smaller—that may help guide whether he or she needs to intervene or not.

CLIMATE SCENARIO TWO
Inconsistent Internet

As technology becomes a bigger part of what the teachers embrace, it should be no surprise that the mood of the school can become dicey when the internet is down. Whether teachers are entering grades or attendance,

continued ⇨

checking emails, using Zoom, or updating a Facebook page, network crashes can seem like they bring a classroom to a halt, if not the whole school.

This is especially true for the teachers who did not build a plan B into their lesson (for example, planning for what to do if the computers crash in the middle of class). And that's exactly what happened at Green Mountain Middle School. Although the staff know this is a temporary problem, it has created a lot of stress and anxiety across the school. This is how you know it is a climate issue; it is temporary. Right now, it seems like the biggest deal in the world, but once the problem is resolved, it will disappear from memory.

When a school has technology issues, it can change the attitudes of the faculty that day. For most, fixing the problem will fix the day as well. For a few people who are looking for excuses not to grow or adapt, it could provide an excuse for not using the technology at all. This is a climate issue that could become a culture issue if leaders ignore it. A principal might wander around the school after the technology issue is fixed to ensure the naysayers do not use this situation as ammunition later (perhaps stating, "See, I told you the administration doesn't care about us"). Keep in mind that something related to climate could potentially influence or become part of the culture if it persists. This can be a good or a bad situation, but it is essential for the leader to be aware of this opportunity to do something or risk doing nothing.

CLIMATE SCENARIO THREE
Motivational Speaker Syndrome

At Pleasant High School it is common for school leaders to start the new year with a motivational speaker; this investment is for the benefit of some of the less engaged staff. Each year, the speaker pushes all the right buttons—teachers laugh, cry, wonder, and leave the session feeling temporarily excited and invigorated. This feeling would last about a day or two, and then everything would return to normal. This is not a dysfunctional school, so "returning to normal" is not necessarily a negative thing. This is an example of how leaders can impact the climate of the school without touching the culture. Staff feel better for a short period of time, the climate changes, but the culture prevails a few days later, and nothing changes.

A school leader who might want to take a new approach to try to move from climate to culture could use this opportunity to reflect on this issue at future meetings, have informal discussions in the hallways, or change a few of his or her behaviors to model what the motivational speaker may have shared. In our experiences, whatever a motivational speaker may talk about only can have traction if the opinion leaders of the faculty want it to. Anyone can change the attitude of a group in the short term; it takes a sustained effort and commitment from school leaders to let that temporary change become the catalyst for a change in the culture (Gruenert & Whitaker, 2019). Typically, these leaders determine if any type of staff development is truly ongoing. They could take something the speaker said that resonated—or that they wanted to resonate—and regularly write about it in staff memos or even adopt it as a motto. This is a way to deepen the climate impact from one-time events to a greater impact.

The Confusion Between Culture and Climate Change

In many schools, we find leaders making great changes to improve. Some of these changes are related to the climate of the school. Unfortunately, many leaders may claim they have changed the culture when actually they only have made a few changes to the climate. We say *only* because relative to a culture change, changing climate is easier. This does not mean it is not important—quite the opposite, but it is a quicker alteration.

The following scenarios may help shed some light on why some educators may become confused about culture versus climate.

SCENARIO ONE
Collaborative Teams for Student Achievement

A small team of high school teachers decided to meet after school to discuss student achievement without any push from the administration—they just wanted to do it. While this may represent a new routine for this team, it does not equal a change in culture. For this to be a culture change, the size of the team would need to be significantly larger, the time period of this new practice would need to extend into a second and third year, and it would become routine to invite new teachers into the process.

A leader could make sure team members become mentors to new teachers, share planning time with them, or have their classrooms in close proximity.

continued ⇨

This could make it easier for the team to grow. Continuing to expand the team could potentially influence the culture if the subculture activities become a normal part of the school. If the team becomes successful enough, it might be easier to have this practice become more of an expectation for the entire school. However, it must be the team that brings the idea to the other faculty.

This scenario demonstrates efforts that started as a climate issue, which evolved into a subculture, and could expand to become part of the school culture. Many changes in a school start at this level, and it is important to understand the next steps.

SCENARIO TWO
Popcorn Machine

The parent-teacher organization recently purchased a popcorn machine for the middle school. Some teachers asked the principal if they could pop popcorn during the day and serve some to students during their classes. After a few weeks and with the principal's OK, many more teachers are doing this and then asked if their students could oversee the cooking and delivery of popcorn to the classrooms. Again, the principal agreed. At this middle school, it is now common to smell popcorn in the hallways in the late mornings and afternoons. Similar to the previous scenario, this is simply a new tradition that supports a need for students that has always been there. Some students get a little hungry in between meals, and the teachers just found a new way to satisfy that need.

No values or beliefs changed. Obviously, the climate will change each time the smell of popcorn is in the air. Students and other faculty may pressure teachers who do not allow popcorn in their classrooms to allow it. The custodial staff is probably a bit more anxious than they were before, given the possibility of more messes around the school.

This activity could become the beginning of a general culture shift as this student need raises the awareness of more teachers and they begin to accommodate students more. Even if this activity goes on for a few years, it may not represent a culture change as much as a *culture affirmation*. The teachers have always valued students; this has become one way to prove it. The culture change would be obvious if the school had a history of ignoring student needs, and the popcorn was one of many changes to meet those needs. A principal can also share success stories from this activity, talk about them at faculty meetings, and so on. This can be a gateway from climate change to culture change if the leader handles it correctly.

This scenario clearly stems from a climate impact—popcorn! The narrow view of popcorn will always remain a climate phenomenon. However, if it expands to focusing on the needs of students—at a variety of levels—the result could be a much broader push toward nudging the culture. If this climate attempt has a negative impact, such as popcorn being thrown on the floor, students being disciplined, custodians having to mop up messes, this could prevent a culture slide in a positive direction.

SCENARIO THREE
Metal Detector on Campus

With the increase of school shootings and violence toward school students and staff, a high school decides to purchase a metal detector with a police officer who monitors it during all school hours and special events for each school.

The need for a safe school has always been there; this is just another way of expressing that value. If the teachers feel using a metal detector is too much, or that its use sends the wrong message regarding how safe (or unsafe) the school is, then this change might not survive. Similar to the two previous scenarios, whenever a school staff chooses to further support an existing value or belief, it is not a culture change; it is the staff's way of saying what is important *now*, even though they have always valued it.

This is an example of how the tone and manner of an event might determine the climate and potentially the culture. If the community or staff raise concerns about the necessity of metal detectors, that is a different result than if it makes everyone feel safer. Always remember, we must handle climate and culture with great care.

SCENARIO FOUR
New Discipline Policy

In an elementary school, classroom management is a rising issue. Teachers are becoming frustrated with student behavior, and the administrators feel limited in how they can respond due to some school board policies. To address this

continued ⇨

issue, the principal decides to convene a committee of teachers, students, and community members with the hope of restructuring the student discipline code and bringing new proposals for the school board's consideration. This is the first time this principal has invited the public to help address a problem at the school.

The committee meets several times over the next few months. Members discuss scenarios and potential repercussions for students. They build a new framework that teachers and administrators can use to hopefully curtail the rising incidents of student misbehavior. The school board is pleased with the new student discipline framework and passes it unanimously.

The committee has a small celebration, and the school staff are now beginning to see differences. This is a great thing for this school. The climate changes. The culture is nudged. This could be the difference between simply adopting a new student discipline policy and actually improving student behavior. The policy change probably impacts climate, but a future improvement in student behavior moves toward a culture change.

One way to think of climate is to realize the interaction between student climate and teacher climate. If discipline is too loose, some students may like it but many teachers will not. Similarly, if the discipline is too strict, some teachers may like it and it could result in improved teacher climate. However, if it is too rigid, it can negatively impact student climate.

The committee from the previous scenario about the new discipline policy did not change the culture; but it did prove to the faculty that they can use this type of activity to solve future problems. Should the faculty default to developing committees that include students and community members to address problems at the school—that would be a change in the culture. A culture change is a change in the way you do things every day—not just a cool thing that happens one time. If you do something once, it impacts the climate. If you never stop, it may impact the culture. Members of a culture usually resist change, and only repeated attempts will break through. Climate changes provides a pathway to get to culture changes.

Doing something new, or doing something for the first time, does not change school culture. It's only when people stop calling it new and start to do it automatically that the culture starts to change. COVID-19 did not change the culture; instead, it revealed it by showing that schools were flexible in meeting students' needs and accommodating distance learning, engaging students in a different way, and so on. We may have talked about doing these things before, but the pandemic actually revealed that it was a part of our culture. The culture has always valued personal and public health, but this crisis gave us a chance to show it.

The following scenario is another example of how a change can feel like a culture shift when it is actually a climate shift. The issue is one that people often mis-categorize between culture and climate—*teacher satisfaction*. Clearly, teacher satisfaction is important and critical to understand, and it gives us a peek into the school culture.

SCENARIO FIVE
Teacher Satisfaction

A middle school principal is struggling with the morale of the adults in his building. This includes teachers, administrative assistants, custodians, cooks, and others. The superintendent is made aware of this issue and challenges the principal to change the "culture of dissatisfaction." As noted previously, a *culture of satisfaction* does not exist in any school. This is a misuse of the term *culture*, but probably means the superintendent wants the principal to address the climate of the building (and does not know the difference between the two concepts).

This principal decides to administer a climate survey that asks staff to respond to questions related to how they feel about the school and which parts of being at school are the most frustrating. This is *climate*—how people feel about things. To change the climate, ask questions related to *climate*, not *culture*. To change culture, ask questions about *culture*, not *climate*. Seems simple enough, but only if you know the difference between the two concepts. The results come back, and an analysis of the data reveals some problems with the conditions of the aging building, outdated technology, and lunch breaks that seem too short. The principal thanks the staff for their responses and shares with them a plan to improve building aesthetics and update technology, as well as build in more time for lunch in the schedule. Immediately, the staff satisfaction levels seem to rise, and the superintendent is happy.

Some might argue the principal changed the culture by improving the morale in the building. It is possible the principal may have established a new routine for addressing issues (administering surveys). But the principal did not touch the culture. In fact, the culture "won," and the climate change was temporary. Dissatisfaction was manifest through the behaviors of the faculty and staff, and the survey affirmed that dissatisfaction. We would argue that throughout the years, whenever there was an issue, the administrators discovered it through the actions of the faculty or staff. There was no other means of sharing problems and chances are, people got in trouble if they complained too much. Making people happier does not change a culture, just like taking aspirin for a headache works for about four hours.

This does not imply it was a mistake to improve faculty and staff satisfaction. There is little benefit in a negative tone in the school. What the survey does provide is a new approach. If the first survey is about climate and the faculty feels heard, they may be more open to honestly sharing about deeper cultural issues and believe that change is a possibility. Sometimes getting an organization moving in *any* direction is the first step toward getting it to move in the *right* direction. Remember, objects at rest stay at rest, and objects in motion stay in motion.

Additional Analogies to Demonstrate the Difference Between Culture and Climate

In the introduction (page 1), we used the following analogy (a virus creating a fever, and then the immune system fighting the fever) to describe the difference between culture and climate. The culture is the immune system, the climate is the fever, and the virus itself is the change. Another helpful analogy for understanding the relationship between culture and climate is to think more specifically in terms of education. If we personify these terms, culture is the personality of the school, and climate is the attitude.

Culture, like someone's personality, is extremely difficult to change. Attitudes, however, can alter moment-to-moment with a number of factors influencing them. School leaders may make minor changes in a school system, and in doing so, they can accidentally step on someone's toes; or in an attempt to please one person, they can damage their relationship with another. We can accidentally forget to thank someone for a great effort or be misunderstood by a teacher when trying to help a student through a disciplinary issue. We are not saying that climate is fragile, rather, just that you can tamper with it as easily as you can fix it. Bringing in donuts can fix just about any school climate issue, and removing donuts may cause a climate issue all its own. You can add jeans days, or you can take them away. Neither one is inherently right nor wrong, but either one can impact the climate.

This is one reason why hiring new staff is a major opportunity to influence culture—the personality of a school. The friends you choose to spend time with can determine the type of person you become. By adding the right people, making sure they have the support they need, and connecting them with the appropriate peers, leaders can start to reimagine their school cultures from the ground up.

If there is a positive culture in an organization, the more effective teachers are usually much more willing and comfortable keeping their doors open so others can see what they are doing. Leaders reinforce and reward positivity—at least informally. If teachers feel threatened because they are in the minority and using ineffective practices, they will not want others to see in their classrooms. In some schools, the less effective teachers shut their doors and there is little conversation about how they teach; to some, it seems rude to intrude. This is an important aspect to think about. If the most successful teachers close their doors and are reluctant to speak about the activities in their classrooms, the principal may have a bigger problem to address. The same goes for sharing ideas and practices in any school setting. If the culture values collaboration, it happens regularly and continues to grow. If it doesn't, innovation quickly dries up. When the environment is one of isolation, the result is that either the most effective teachers do not share or the least effective do not grow, or both. This can have the opposite effect of a collaborative culture, which of course, is much more desirable.

Another analogy is to think of culture as a bathtub full of ice. Psychologist Kurt Lewin's (1951) change model talks of *frozen* systems and the need to *unfreeze* them so change can take place. We like to think of the culture as a bathtub that is completely full of frozen water without room to add anything else without something spilling out. Of course, no spillage (change) is possible without thawing out the water first. So, now imagine the tub is full of water, not frozen, meaning it is now vulnerable to change due to, for example, hiring a new principal, changing school policies, or grappling with a pandemic (yes, the pandemic did create an opportunity to change the culture, but it did not change). Just think how often we have heard people say they want to return to normal. Normal is the culture calling us back.

Think of any kind of change, whether it be personnel, scheduling, rituals, or routines *as cups of water* (or perhaps bigger changes as buckets of water). Add those to the tub, and what happens? Some of the water spills out due to displacement. The culture can only hold so much. Whatever spills out is hopefully something that was not critical to the effectiveness of the school. Unfortunately, you cannot predict or guarantee what will happen when you mess with culture in a clumsy way. This same thing occurs when adding a new employee. If you replace a negative staff member with a positive one, it can be quite impactful on the temperature (or climate)—it can thaw things. Each positive voice can join a subculture that can lead to significant school change. However, if you just hire someone randomly, nothing is likely to get better and you might as well have kept the water frozen.

If culture is a tub full of water, then the climate is the temperature of the water. Climate in this analogy will determine whether change is welcome or not, and whether the culture is vulnerable to change. In this analogy, climate plays a bigger role than in previous examples. Climate might freeze or thaw the culture, depending on the type of change coming and what you have done in the past when attempting this type of change.

Realize that if you carefully remove enough water, it will still create a void, but the leader can now control what goes back in. However, this definitely takes a deft touch, not an oversized ladle. Think of improving climate as adding warmer water to change the temperature of the tub water. You must consistently do it, or the impact is quickly lost. In the same way changing the culture is not a one-off event, nor is changing the climate.

When does it matter to know the difference between culture and climate? When you ask yourself the following self-reflection questions.

1. "Why has our workplace productivity changed?"
2. "How do we improve our workplace productivity?"

Basically, when workplace productivity changes, you'll want to know if it is a spike, a dip, or a new normal. Knowing the difference between culture and climate gives educators the precision they need to address issues correctly. This precision gives you the language you need to locate the cause and fix it. It is essential that leaders notice trends. Are things getting better or worse? Which people are becoming more comfortable, and which are becoming less comfortable? Who is closing their doors to outsiders?

If you have a problem with workplace productivity, you can usually narrow it down to one of two reasons: (1) *staff can't get better* due to barriers that were not there before; it is not a choice, or 2) *staff won't change* because they don't want to; it is a choice they are making. Stating you cannot get better, or stating you won't change is something a culture that has been in place for a long time supports. Stating they cannot get better is not something new teachers express at faculty meetings, nor do they announce this during their interviews. All the logic, data, and confrontation will not change a culture in place for a long time. Leaders must show people where the organization is relative to where they want the organization to be, a new perspective that shows what the staff have to lose. And understand, the culture, not the climate, will fight this new perspective. The climate will be a potential resource in building this perspective. Know the difference.

Knowing the difference between school culture and climate is important, but educators should understand the commonalities as well.

The Commonalities of School Culture and Climate

The biggest thing culture and climate have in common is their elusiveness. They are social constructs that people create to represent collective values, beliefs, and feelings. Both are projections of who people are and which groups they belong to. Ultimately, both provide direction for how people will spend their energy and time. For either to change, we need to change our minds. The real challenge for school leaders is changing other people's minds.

To change a person's mind, we need to tell different stories (Godin, 2012). Stories get into our heads and shape our beliefs and values. It may sound simple, yet there is a deep complexity to this challenge. Who tells the story, when they tell it, how often they tell it, and so much more, all matter when you really dig into shaping a culture.

Stories can change a climate, and stories are what ultimately change cultures. Someone can tell a story about another teacher, about the football team, or about the new principal, and chances are, people will react with emotion. One of the tools in the leader's toolbox should be storytelling. Change the climate with a good story. Change the culture by telling that same story again and again.

Conclusion

Culture and climate are inevitably linked, but they are very different. Climate can, and will, change from day to day; however, this does not mean it can't be impacted on a longer-term basis. The climate of a school can trend in an up or down direction. Thus, the impact can be extended with the correct care and nurturing. However, school climate may be one of the best ways to influence school culture. By setting a positive tone (climate) each day, the climate has a chance to alter the long-term dynamics of school (culture). Recognizing the differences as well as the interrelationships between culture and climate is an essential component of improving schools and classrooms.

CHAPTER 3

Elements of Climate

When considering the differences between culture and climate, we found it difficult to pin down any aspects of climate until we started using terms such as *satisfaction, loyalty,* and *morale*. After adding *attitude* and *attendance* to this mix, we realized that these are also some of the climate elements educators most commonly misattribute to culture—the imposters of culture. Too often, school leaders who are asked to fix short-term problems that are part of the climate will claim they have fixed the culture. There is nothing wrong with fixing problems; educators just need to seek more precision in what is actually happening.

Elements of Climate Versus Elements of Culture

We developed table 3.1 to differentiate between the *elements of culture* and the *elements of climate*. Hopefully, this list will further elucidate the differences between the two concepts. Because these elements will have some overlap, this list is primarily a theoretical one—in the absence of quantitative research, it will likely remain that way.

Table 3.1: Elements of Culture and Climate

ELEMENTS OF CULTURE	ELEMENTS OF CLIMATE
Climate	Satisfaction
Mission	Morale
Vision	Attitude
Tools	Loyalty

continued ⇨

ELEMENTS OF CULTURE	ELEMENTS OF CLIMATE
Language	Attendance
Rituals, routines, and ceremonies	
Stories	
Norms	
Values	
Beliefs	
Symbols	
Heroes	

Source: Gruenert & Whitaker, 2015.

The following elements of climate are helpful as lenses through which educators can view their school.

- **Satisfaction:** It can be difficult to assess satisfaction with any group in the throes of change. To be satisfied with uncertainty—which comes with any change—does not seem logical. Leaders should measure satisfaction well *after* implementing the change to assess if it's working—if it made things better. They can measure satisfaction as a way to determine if change is supporting their most effective teachers. Typically, the most effective teachers want growth and improvement, and they know that some level of unknown is acceptable to accomplish them. It's generally the less effective teachers who struggle the most with change. It can be scary. If ineffective teachers seem satisfied, then the change may not be what you had hoped for. So, it becomes more important to know *who* is satisfied rather than getting an overall assessment of the faculty and staff.

  When people are satisfied in a place where they were unsatisfied before, it does not mean the culture changed. The opposite is also true; if people who were once satisfied are not now, this does not mean the culture changed. In both situations, it is possible the culture is changing, but the levels of satisfaction did not change the culture. A change in satisfaction is simply an indicator that something is happening—much like a person having a fever. The fever did not cause the virus. However, clearly something is happening to the climate. The duration and consistency of this climate change will be a likely determining factor to see if it can begin to impact the culture. Satisfaction is more about how we feel than what we believe.

- **Morale:** Morale and satisfaction are very similar in that they both provide signals regarding the overall health of the school, but both can be misleading. If toxic people are satisfied, something is off; and when morale is high due to dedication to the wrong things or people, it may be time for the leader to step in. Morale is usually high if the job is satisfying, but morale also could be high if the leader does not expect teachers to do much. Keeping an eye on the morale of the adults in the school building helps leaders know if the climate is changing.

  Think about a school with an emotionally absent leader. Less effective staff may initially welcome this leader, as it allows them to proceed unchallenged. The more effective staff, however, will eventually feel frustrated that this leader will allow less effective staff to continue to negatively impact students and the school. This is one reason it is essential to continually monitor how the most positive, capable and productive staff feel. If they are unhappy, typically something significant is wrong with the school. Having a big-picture mindset makes more effective teachers great barometers for the health of the school. The morale of both the less effective and more effective teachers, just like with satisfaction, can tell leaders much about where the school culture is and also possibly where it is heading. Morale, like climate, can change quickly, unlike culture.

- **Attitude:** Climate in general represents the attitude of the organization, whereas culture represents the personality (Gruenert & Whitaker, 2015). Let's take this one step further. To maintain good standing in a culture, it is not the leader's attitude that matters; it is the attitude others *expect* the leader to have that matters. Some events will evoke certain responses, depending on the climate. For example, the mere mention of professional development inspires groans from some educators, often due to recurring patterns of past tedious or unhelpful professional development activities. In these situations, new teachers may quickly learn that when the principal announces a professional development opportunity, some veteran teachers expect everyone to roll their eyes and try to avoid participating. In schools with more effective cultures, teachers might view professional development as an exciting opportunity to improve their skills or help students.

New teachers look forward to the activities and note that veteran teachers value them, so they should too.

It's the culture that causes educators to act this way—to adopt certain attitudes—and the culture justifies those sentiments with a shared history of events that have grown to define the next experience. Some staff and teachers look forward to or value the chance to learn, grow, and interact with their peers. Yet, in some schools, teachers are not supposed to like professional development—and the pressure to conform is there regardless; play the game or lose your membership. Teachers learn attitudes.

It's important to note that leaders cannot change a culture without involving professional development. Professional development is a strong factor in forming collaborative school cultures. The attitudes of staff reveal a lot about the culture, yet staff attitudes can change and usually do because the culture demands it as a form of self-defense or conforming to the established norms. Any change of attitude is usually not a surprise as much as it is an effort to fit in with the crowd.

- **Loyalty:** Many leaders cherish loyalty. Some would rank it above competence when determining who to hire. Think of *loyalty* as an over-commitment to something or someone that causes people to stay the course when evidence suggests there may be a problem doing so. Typically, leaders earn loyalty, and when it seems that loyalty is getting stronger or weaker, some may argue the culture is changing, but that's not necessarily true.

  A true test may be whether the person is loyal to students, the organization, or an individual leader. When an organization's culture includes loyalty to the students or school, that culture has a greater chance of doing great things for students. If the culture centers on the personality of a leader, the overall climate may be far more volatile.

  Actually, when loyalty wanes, it's a signal that the leaders have not represented the culture's values and beliefs well. This type of school may have people who are loyal to *ideas* rather than the leader. In other words, find people who can become loyal to a mission, a vision, or their reference group rather than the leader, and improvement becomes a more aggressive pursuit.

- **Attendance:** For our purposes, *attendance* is not only physically or virtually being present but being present mentally and emotionally as well. This goes beyond contrived participation. It is a form of active involvement in the day-to-day events in the organization that is obvious to others, perhaps no more so than through body language. This is why many leaders who host Zoom meetings or online events ask everyone to turn on their cameras.

Thinking about attendance in this context tells leaders something about the climate of the school, as this type of attendance reveals the quality of teacher and staff engagement, whatever the activity. If the school culture values professional development, attendance at these events will reflect levels of buy-in and confidence that faculty and staff cannot hide or fake. Being an element of climate, attendance can change rather quickly depending on the teachers' attitudes, satisfaction levels, or morale. The culture will ultimately show teachers and staff which events are worth attending, as well as how to act at these events.

The purpose in recognizing these constructs as elements of climate is not to discount their value toward improving schools. These elements serve as indicators of the type of culture you may have relative to the culture you want. During any cultural change, these elements will change—some more than others, which could help gauge the pace of change, and let you know when to push on, or when to slow down.

School leaders should understand that when the culture changes, these climate elements will also change. However, when these climate elements change, it doesn't always mean the culture is changing. Attitudes might change many times each day, but that does not mean personalities are changing. Levels of satisfaction, morale, loyalty, and attendance are reflections of the cultural norms in the school. Leaders enforce these norms. Leaders do not set the tone, but whoever sets the tone is the leader.

Also, staff acting more positive—or at least acting less negative—may not seem significant, but it does allow new staff to form their own opinions and attitudes instead of immediately conforming. If you ever wonder about the influence of culture, just remember that no collegiate teacher preparation program has a course on griping in the teachers' lounge, but some master it after only a couple of months in the school. Similarly, some staff may have natural negative attitudes, but because of the positive tone set by others in the school, they choose not to manifest them. This is the power of culture.

School Climate as a Tool

Think of climate as one of many tools in the culture toolbox. You can add things to the toolbox—up to a point. A toolbox can get full or become obsolete as you need different tools. A quick look at a tool catalog from 1970 will show many tools people no longer use, or a website dedicated to tools may show many tools people have never heard of or that are specific to particular jobs. People often buy tools they may never use more than once and others they may use quite often.

The toolbox rarely changes and hardly ever gets thrown away. If a new problem arises, we usually end up buying a new tool. Changing the culture is usually overkill when dealing with most issues. People rarely, if ever, change the whole culture (or toolbox); instead, we change the climate (or tools).

You use tools to fix problems, however, problems can be persistent. For every problem, there usually is a *happy person* hoping the problem stays. For example, if you are the second-slowest runner on the track team, you probably don't want the slowest person to improve. This sheds some light on why many problems are difficult to fix. Some problems can hang around for such a long time that people no longer consider them problems; they become a part of who they are and what they accept. Actually, cultures *need* problems because cultures are frameworks for solving problems (Deal & Peterson, 1999). So, if you don't have any problems, a culture might not be necessary. A culture will not grow very quickly or become very strong without a reason to exist.

Problems tend to persist when there are people who benefit from them. For example, when a school over-identifies students with special needs, it can create many new demands and adjustments as well as some additional financial funding. Yet a school may also blame the special education program for its lack of success. All the changes and adjustments may create a difficult place to work. Having a built-in excuse (problem) can buy a lot of forgiveness from the community when the faculty and staff tell the story that way: "We have so many students with special needs, we cannot improve test scores." Having big problems that never go away tends to lower the bar and provide members of that culture permission to do nothing about them. This can lead to *high* levels of satisfaction, morale, and loyalty, even though the members of that culture know in their hearts that they need to fix several issues.

This same thing can occur when we look at test scores and other numerical information. We have the same toolbox, but we may have to choose different tools. School leaders might choose to look at the tools of climate (attitudes, attendance, loyalty, and so on) to analyze what is happening as well as determine the first steps toward resolution. Student data is important, but it is not the only tool that matters.

Whenever you look at data, assuming they are accurate, you are looking into a mirror. When you do not like what you see in the mirror, you don't fix the mirror. Mirrors, like data, don't lie. School leaders often want to present a positive outlook of their schools regardless of any negative information they learn. There is nothing wrong with leaders having an optimistic disposition. The challenge comes when they receive data that do not speak well of the school or the leaders, or when they cover up problems with an overabundance of optimism (Sibony, 2020). Leaders can build loyalty when they create an environment in which others don't need to worry about solving problems. When things go bad in negative organizations, it is easy for staff to become dismissive or defensive, or start pointing fingers.

When a school presents the data representing the culture, we try not to focus on the negative. In our experiences helping schools navigate challenging cultures, we find few school leaders willing to admit there is a problem. The more effective leaders own the problems. When we challenge ineffective or struggling schools, there is a tendency for leaders to reveal loyalties to faculty and staff for the wrong reasons. Some leaders may not want us back, which is a pretty common phenomenon. In any school, there will be strengths and challenges related to its culture. One unproductive practice we witnessed was a leader focusing too much energy on trying to fix the climate, assuming that would fix the culture. He was fixated on keeping the faculty happy.

Doing the wrong thing is worse than doing nothing. If school leaders attempt to make changes to the culture without knowing all this may involve, they can make a negative culture stronger, with the leaders on the outside looking in. People become defensive when they feel threatened or when they sense someone is trying to convince them of something (Cialdini, 2016). When working with school leaders, if we discount their current culture, these leaders can easily take this as a personal insult.

If you think of climate as the tool you use to solve problems, then it is only a "problem" when you try to use it to fix problems that require a different tool. It's like trying to drive a nail into a piece of wood using a screwdriver. There are plenty of jobs climate is not the best tool for. For example, climate does not help leaders reveal their hidden assumptions about teaching and learning, a very critical component to address when trying to change how educators teach. Try to imagine climate as a tool to fix something rather than as something that needs to be fixed.

Conclusion

Discussing the elements of both culture and climate may be the best way to describe the differences between them. Climate is an element of culture, and climate has elements within it that pretend to be elements of the culture without actually being so. Culture is the toolbox, and elements of the climate are the tools in that toolbox that educators can use to solve problems in the school. These elements include satisfaction, morale, attitude, loyalty, and attendance, among others.

We are not suggesting that issues like satisfaction, morale, or loyalty are unimportant—they are ways of revealing the climate in a school and possibly levers you can use to change a climate. Ultimately, climate is a tool of culture. While we call it an element, understanding it as a tool might make more sense to those who wish to improve their school culture.

CHAPTER 4

Classroom Cultures

Do classrooms really have their own cultures? Each classroom has what feels a lot like a culture, and for the purposes of this chapter, we'll use the term *classroom culture*. However, each classroom *definitely* has a climate that may vary from day to day. In most schools, the makeup of the students is unique from year to year and maybe even from grading period to grading period, so establishing a classroom culture can be a challenge.

The classroom culture allows for much quicker alterations than an entire school, which typically has the vast majority of same staff members from year to year. If teachers want a different culture each year, it is at least partially up to them. For the most part, their new students have little or no knowledge of past norms, rules, or expectations, so the classroom dynamic is still unmolded. Some high school teachers will see the same students a few times since they may teach different courses. And, it may be that there are smaller, independent classroom cultures in your school, which we explore in the next section.

The purpose of this chapter is to help readers understand how the concept of organizational culture manifests itself at the classroom level, and to present a typology of potential classroom cultures. We will show where classroom cultures come from and what might influence them using relatable examples and scenarios. Most important, we want to show teachers how classroom-level efficacy is achievable even when it feels as though the walls are closing in.

The Small Culture

All classrooms will have the feeling of a culture, intended or not, good or bad. But also consider the possibility that a school may have a number of distinct smaller cultures operating inside it. Is it possible for a small group of people to have a culture of its own not connected to the larger school culture? Anyone who's stepped into the classroom of a particularly strong or weak teacher knows this can be the case—the room simply operates on a different level from the rest of the school. This is a *small culture*, while the school culture is a larger culture. The two cultures will interact, but the small culture is different from what one might consider a *subculture*, which is "an ethnic, regional, economic, or social group exhibiting characteristic patterns of behavior sufficient to distinguish it from others within an embracing culture or society" ("Subculture," n.d.). It's important to differentiate between small cultures and subcultures. The small culture has little connection with the larger culture, whereas the subculture is a direct byproduct of the larger culture.

Consider a small group of people at a local church who have become a bit annoyed with the way things have been going there. This might be a bible study or Sunday school group. This group may decide to have small meetings at someone's home to discuss the issues, and some may even approach the leadership of the church with their concerns. Most of the time, it ends there. The church leadership either responds to grievances or denies the calls for change. Sometimes, however, the small group may decide to build its own church. While groups of teachers are unlikely to declare independence from the school they work for, the impact of *cultural secession* on a school can be immense.

A classroom might become a small, somewhat independent group that develops unique rituals, routines, ceremonies, and norms. This would be typical of a weak school culture; *weak* meaning the overall school culture does not impose itself on what happens in classrooms. Weak does not always imply ineffective. A teacher may lead his or her students into what feels like a private club, full of stories, rites, and traditions that glorify the classroom. Whenever a group embraces these elements, we call it a *small culture*.

What, then, makes any of this distinct from subcultures? Simply put, *subcultures* need more autonomy than most classrooms can achieve in a school. Perhaps all small cultures start as small groups of people who develop into a clique, then into a subculture, and then some move into a system that becomes independent of the original, larger culture. Certainly, a classroom culture would still have some give and take with the school culture, regardless of the level of separation a teacher might try to create. Think of classrooms as the different boroughs of New York City—all distinct yet interconnected.

The implications of having small cultures in your school may initially seem innocuous. Even if the small cultures are the result of great teachers going unique ways, dividing your school into a number of different *fiefdoms* will still strain the organizational culture in the long run. If some teachers feel the need to create small, separate cultures, something is wrong with the school culture.

Classroom Culture as a Reflection of Teacher Attitude and Mindset

The easiest way to describe *classroom culture* is to think about the elements that make up a culture: values, beliefs, language, rituals, and so on. Each classroom will have these elements that help differentiate it from all other classrooms. Many culture elements that exist at the building level will have some influence on the classroom-level elements. Once teachers become aware of how their classroom cultures frame students' behaviors, they can begin to orchestrate those elements to support and influence a more effective classroom culture.

You can usually sense a certain feeling when walking into any classroom, often the setting is unique to the rest. The décor, furniture arrangement, teacher's vocal inflection, instructional activities, and student behavior all provide the essence of a distinct classroom culture. If educators choose to ignore this phenomenon, they may be missing out on one of the biggest factors that influence the quality of instruction (Buchanan-Rivera, 2017). This is where teacher effectiveness comes in. If a particular approach requires hands-on learning, but the teacher keeps the desks in rows, this may directly impact the quality of instruction and learning. Similarly, if a teacher focuses too much on instructor-centered instruction, it can diminish student growth by reducing their mental processing. Soon the school culture will begin providing a recipe for what learning looks like at the school, and most teachers will adopt it. Listen to the veteran teacher who walks into the new teacher's classroom for the first time.

What teachers do in the classroom ultimately determines the quality of education students receive. Just as school cultures are extensions of the principal's personality (Deal & Peterson, 2016), the same is true of teachers and their classrooms. The teacher's values and beliefs establish the essence of the classroom's culture. The culture sets the rules and unwritten rules for those who enter the classroom. Classroom culture may be one of the strongest factors that differentiates effective teachers from ineffective teachers, but it's also one of the most difficult to identify.

Let's take a look at unwritten rules. In secondary schools, student tardiness can be a nagging issue. Whether or not the class or the entire school has a definition of what *tardy* means, doesn't each class have its own unwritten rule? Is a student on time when he or she is in the room, in his or her seat? Does it depend on who the student is or the mood of the teacher?

What about inappropriate behavior in general? Does the class understand when a student has crossed the line? Does it depend on who the student is or what day of the week it is? Is the teacher consistent from day to day, or does his or her attitude depend on how far off the next three-day weekend is?

If the concept of unwritten rules is salient to effective teaching, we could argue that some classroom cultures are more effective than others in accomplishing this. For example, if the teacher is consistent in allowing or not allowing talking, discussing, and answering questions, regardless of what the rules are, the unwritten rules will trump any posted or announced expectations. What happens in individual classrooms could create a collective "common sense" approach to teaching, eventually leading to a set of norms within a school, but these norms should not create a prescription for all classrooms if they are ineffective.

Picture a high school teacher who sees how his or her first-hour class greatly differs from his or her third-hour class. It could be because of the makeup of the students, size of the classes, or something else entirely. But usually a teacher's first-hour class is more similar to his or her third-hour class than to another teacher's first-hour class in the school. Additionally, even though they may feel different from year to year, most teachers' classes will be more similar to theirs from the previous year than they are to another teacher's classes. This can change, but typically it does not vary by much. These same differences apply to leaders. They may feel that different schools take various approaches, but typically a school feels very similar when the same principal moves to a different building. Such unwritten rules travel with the principal just like they usually move with the teacher.

The power of culture is in the latent qualities that meet peoples' needs; people typically do not feel the influence of culture and will operate in a default mode others introduce to them as they are socialized into the system. However, once a teacher has an idea of what organizational culture is, and what his or her classroom culture looks like, the teacher may begin the process of shaping a more effective classroom culture. Teachers will realize they have a choice. Fully understanding culture provides teachers with a sense of what type of classroom they may have relative to the type of classroom they *could* have or *want* to have. Most teachers believe that whatever they do in their classrooms is effective, although they rarely get a chance to observe other classrooms or watch other teachers teach. They typically don't know how they are doing compared to everyone else in the school.

In any classroom, given enough time, patterns of behavior evolve, expectations emerge, and teachers establish norms and creates rules in response to those behaving outside the norms. There are rewards for following rules and sanctions for those breaking rules. U.S. educators traditionally value students sitting quietly in their seats. Traditional teachers praise this behavior and punish students unable to conform to this expectation. The teachers reinforce values—the aspects of the classroom experience that matter the most—through rituals such as taking attendance or giving awards for compliance.

Eventually, the classroom will take on an idiosyncratic quality—although it usually will not be too far removed from the school's culture. A local vocabulary emerges that helps define membership in a particular classroom. Class members share stories and jokes that define desired behaviors through declared heroes (students who have done great things), affirmed values, and membership confirmations in this group. In some classrooms, students fit in if they try and care. In others, goofing around is the accepted and expected standard. Once this becomes clear, it is easy to see how students become members in the classroom culture. Assumptions that drive behavior gradually become latent. The classroom culture is beginning to become established, potentially within a few months or even weeks of the start of the school year, and students begin to behave on autopilot when they enter the room. And the teacher will behave according to the unique culture of each classroom.

If you follow a middle or high school student around for a day, you will quickly notice how he or she behaves differently walking into each classroom. A small portion of this may be due to which peers are in the room, but the vast majority is based on the teacher. This indicates that students are not the variable in the evolution of a classroom's culture. If you want to see this for yourself, watch students on the first day of school. A student enters each classroom in a similar fashion, cautious and wondering about the expectations, rules, and norms. As these elements become more obvious, students will alter their behavior from class to class as soon as they enter each room. Cultures shape students far more than students shape cultures.

One critical classroom culture element is beliefs, also called *assumptions*. Simply put, *assumptions* are what people assume to be true. Schein (2009) states that assumptions are the deepest level of any culture. Assumptions might be thought of as acted-on beliefs, beliefs that seem to be the strongest. You might assume that the teacher who speaks the loudest at faculty meetings represents the whole faculty or at least a large group of colleagues. You also might assume that the more the school pays a teacher, the better job he or she will do. Assumptions are very difficult to articulate because of how deeply rooted they are (Schein, 2009, 2017). However, once teachers examine their assumptions, they will gain a deeper understanding about who they are and how they think, dress, talk, move among students, and react to crises, which can facilitate or inhibit student success.

Teachers' knowledge and beliefs play an essential role in their practices and shape the learning in their classrooms (Bauch, 1984; Borko & Putnam, 1995). In other words, "teachers hold the authority to shape the social conditions of the classroom. Since those conditions help to shape what the children learn about in school, teachers need to be critical of their existing school practice" (Florio-Ruane, 2001, p. 7). Given the social nature of learning, it's no surprise that patterns of behavior evolve uniquely in each classroom. Whether teachers realize it or not, unwritten rules develop that affect the quality of learning in their classroom (Shapiro, 2000). Teachers determine the culture of each classroom, regardless of their intentions to do so.

Similar to an ethnographer, teachers must understand classroom dynamics related to learning through a cultural lens. An *ethnographer* is "a person who studies and describes the culture of a particular society or group" ("Ethnographer" n.d.). Ethnographers can be quite extensive and comprehensive as they analyze a culture. They are trained to view things objectively and record observations without passing judgment, which is rigorous and time consuming. Teachers tend to miss the underlying cultural influence because it has become so familiar to them (Florio-Ruane, 2001). Consequently, they can't identify "patterns of classroom life which often become invisible because they become so regular, patterned, and ordinary" (Frank, 1999, p. 3). Yet, once a teacher identifies these patterns, the subtle nuances that filter his or her thinking and impact behaviors are no longer as elusive or powerful. Understanding these elements means no longer being powerless under their influence.

A Typology of Classroom Cultures

Some teachers may be shocked to hear that their classroom culture is a reflection of their personality. This section describes a typology of eight potential classroom cultures, although there may well be hundreds. Working from the theoretical foundations presented in the School Culture Typology Activity in *School Culture Rewired* (Gruenert & Whitaker, 2015), which establishes six types of school cultures, this classroom culture typology builds around the notion of a collaborative culture as the optimal culture. The point of providing this typology is not so much for you to identify a specific typology as an exact match as much as it is to identify traits and practices of certain classroom cultures, and determine which seem to align best with what is happening in a particular classroom before taking steps to create a better one. This is a way to become aware of the invisible patterns and nuances that shape your classroom. Doing this activity may help you discover some traits from each type that might exist (to some degree) in all of your classrooms, good or bad. We hope teachers understand that the nuances of what happens in a classroom carry a message that transcends whatever they may be teaching that day. The goal is for nobody to feel stuck with what he or she has.

The classroom cultures in this typology are not absolutes, and some of them will sound like generalizations. The purpose, however, isn't precise identification; it's to inspire self-reflection about your own classroom culture. There may be parts of several classroom cultures that resonate with you, and parts of others that you can use for comparison. It would be rare for anyone to have just one type of classroom culture, thus, we allow for many types to inform any teacher's work. Some types will overlap. We have tried to categorize the things we know that happen in classrooms that, in the past, have been hiding or denied discussion.

There are many elements of culture, and some of these may impact the teaching and learning process more than others. For teachers, it is important to be able to scrutinize their classroom culture. They need a common language for being aware of the elements that compose a culture, along with the knowledge that the classroom culture is an extension of their personality.

For the purpose of this chapter, we identify eight general types of classroom cultures, although there are many others we could include. The common thread is that while we tend to teach as we were taught, the school's culture will interact with the teacher's personality and create a response to the work environment that may look like survival more than anything else. Figure 4.1 (page 58) gives a brief overview of each type.

The descriptions are not meant to be judgmental. They are generalizations, and all teachers and classrooms won't fit neatly into these categories. They are a guideline for self-reflection and hope for building a better understanding of classroom culture. They also might help you realize how the roles and relationships among the teachers and the principal in a school develop and evolve.

Traditional Culture

Traditional teachers create a classroom culture that may be a reminder of classrooms from their own days as a student. Their teaching methods may have been most effective early in their careers; however, as times changed, these teachers did

Classroom Culture	Classroom Traits	Teacher Traits
Traditional	• Students are passive recipients of knowledge. • They remind people of classrooms from the past. • The principal is expected to punish students when they misbehave. • Student feelings don't have much connection with their ability to learn.	• Veteran teachers held in high regard • Grade on a curve • Entitled to respect • Stringent regarding student behavior and discipline
Independent	• The classroom door is usually closed. • Principals respect classroom autonomy and leave these teachers alone. • Outside news or information is not usually welcome.	• Keep all personal life issues out of the classroom • Consider autonomy as true measure of a great teacher • Can handle any class and are reluctant to share secrets with colleagues
Warm and Fuzzy	• Emotional and needy students gravitate toward this kind of culture. • Disruptive students are counseled many times before being sent to the office. • They are nice and harmonious places for students to be.	• Don't allow anyone to be critical of others • Use rewards and awards to recognize students' accomplishments and general compliance • Feel the need to make other teachers, students, or parents feel good about themselves • Are team players; the school can depend on them to get things done • Support almost everything the principal wants to do
Collaborative	• Classroom activities infuse authentic, active student engagement. • The principal learns a lot from these classrooms and may use them as examples. • Strong mutual trust exists among students.	• Are aware of the impact of working in teams and how external factors influence the quality of education, especially the impact other teachers have on the success of the whole student • Have a collective sense of responsibility toward ensuring students get the best experiences at and away from school • Are risk takers with a healthy dose of skepticism
Organic	• Student expression is more important than any other aspect of the curriculum.	• Have a Zen quality about them that can cause classroom experiences to transcend the specified curriculum

	• Struggling students seem to do well in this culture and often seek the teacher's personal opinions. • The principal may consider these classrooms effective since they provide an oasis for the discipline-problem students.	• Take class time for students to discuss their personal problems • Expend a lot of energy getting struggling or "problem" students to trust them • Understand the power of mentoring • Have little respect for traditions, finding most obsolete
Helpless	• Students are in control most of the time. • Students get the teacher off track fairly easily, and at times may waste a whole class period. • More often than not, these classrooms are somewhat noisy and chaotic. • Students are sent to the office on a regular basis.	• Believe trust is an important commodity but find it difficult to build • Have loyalty to the strongest person, usually (but not always) the principal • Take it personally if other teachers criticize them in any capacity or offer help without asking first
Toxic	• Culture is not very conducive for learning. • Students dislike coming to class, and some may look for ways to get sent to the office or hallway.	• Are the first to blame new programs, students, other teachers, or the principal when something goes wrong • Feel students often take advantage of them and can have a victim mentality • Have low levels of trust • Apply rules inconsistently, depending on their mood or which students they are dealing with • Enjoy sharing past failures of the school • Can be arrogant and condescending, especially to those who choose not to join them
Burned Out	• Culture is usually an unhappy place until Friday. • Student trust is a luxury *other* teachers have that permits students to get away with more and do less.	• Find it challenging to pretend they like the job, the school, or even students • Have forgotten why they became teachers • May have once been successful but are now tired of trying to be nice • Feel like they have given the system their best shot and lost

Figure 4.1: Eight types of classroom cultures.

*Visit **go.SolutionTree.com/schoolimprovement** for a free reproducible version of this figure.*

not necessarily alter their approaches. For example, they may believe student talking must be kept to a minimum for learning to occur, and all grading is on a curve. They perceive trust as a form of respect they are entitled to from their position rather than one they need to earn. How students feel should not have much connection with their ability to teach or learn. These teachers assume they gain little substance when addressing the *affective domain*, which includes feelings, emotions, attitudes, and the way people deal with things emotionally. This sentiment may carry over into their interactions with adults.

Traditional teachers may believe that students' opinions of one another should not change what happens in the classroom; in fact, this behavior may drive the teacher to become more stringent as overly friendly behaviors emerge. Traditional teachers' classrooms are places where students are passive recipients of knowledge. Any sign of humor, unless the teacher commands it, might be perceived as weak instruction. Laughing in class is usually seen as a sign of off-task behavior.

According to traditional teachers, the role of the principal is to keep discipline using law and order so teaching can occur without unnecessary distractions. They expect the principal to punish students they send to the office, perhaps returning to the classroom, looking down and depressed. These teachers view any contributions from the principal beyond this service as an annoyance or interference.

Traditional teachers believe veteran teachers should be held in the highest regard since they have experienced (or suffered) the most. Traditional teachers tend to love school traditions, as these events tend to become sacred displays of what the school values. They will have classroom traditions as well. Traditional teachers are generally not big risk takers. They may have achieved longevity or tenure by making selective friends in the community, avoiding conflicts, and taking the well-worn path of least resistance.

Other educators, parents, or students may view traditional teachers as arrogant or condescending as they go about the building, assuming informal leadership roles, accrued through referent or expert power (French & Raven, 1959). Some traditional teachers may have charismatic qualities that allow them to form cliques of teachers who can identify with the sentiment of a back-to-basics or no-nonsense approach to education. They typically prefer not to work with organic teachers, which we describe on page 58.

Traditional teachers may have a secret passion for the classrooms of the past, with students needing permission to do anything, seeing the value of an autocratic approach. They may be more systematic in process than systemic in thinking.

Independent Culture

Independent teachers create a classroom culture that attempts to keep all personal lives out of the classroom. The task at hand is to educate students relative to the prescribed curriculum. Discussions of activities outside the classroom (for example, athletics, other teachers, community events) are kept to a minimum, not so much for the sake of learning the curriculum, but rather to keep personal opinions and experiences from interfering with what happens in that classroom. Teachers may disregard students who attempt to share news of happenings around the school, and they may deem this information irrelevant to the class.

The classroom door is usually shut. Independent teachers do not consider trust an important ingredient for success. Similar to the traditional teacher, an *independent teacher* believes autonomy is the true measure of a great teacher and expects to receive it. These teachers can usually handle any class. They eventually figure out what works on their own and are reluctant to share these secrets with other teachers. How they teach is nobody's business as long as it works.

The principal may regard independent teachers as strong educators and comply with their preference for being left alone since things—especially student behaviors—could be worse with a less effective teacher. Their classes are rarely out of control, and they rarely (if ever) send students to the office. The independent teacher has a life away from school and values this time, and he or she often avoids opportunities to spend time with the staff or students away from the classroom or school. These teachers may come across as arrogant or condescending, simply as a defense mechanism to discourage potential friendships within the school. The neediness of helpless teachers (which we discuss later) tends to annoy independent teachers.

Independent teachers may have had role models who were constantly working at their desks or at home, without the help of others, determined to show the world they can do it alone. Autonomy is the key to success, while needing help is a sign of weakness. They loathe any form of collaboration.

Warm and Fuzzy Culture

Emotional and needy students gravitate toward *warm and fuzzy* classroom cultures. In this classroom, students may sway the teacher to discuss personal matters rather than the prescribed curriculum. Warm and fuzzy teachers try not to push students too far beyond the typical amount of work. Teacher expectations are usually based on the current capacity of the class. This teacher doesn't allow anyone to be critical of others. It is a safe place to care.

Warm and fuzzy teachers use rewards and awards to recognize students' accomplishments and general compliance, so students expect them. These expectations may result in these rewards and awards eventually losing some value in other classrooms. Warm and fuzzy teachers feel the need to make other teachers, students, or parents feel good about themselves. Conversations with these teachers might not feel authentic at times due to their need to avoid conflict. They have a very strong need for everyone to like them, as that context seems to prevent a lot of hurt feelings.

Warm and fuzzy teachers will support almost everything the principal wants to do and encourages others to get on board. They counsel disruptive students many times before sending them to the office. These teachers feel a sense of responsibility for any student misbehavior. They are cheerleaders at faculty meetings and in the hallways during school. They believe it is important to keep students happy throughout the day and greet them in the morning. They tend to bring food for other teachers to keep the peace or perhaps celebrate something. They believe that it is not worth the trouble to change any traditions if it seems people will become upset.

Warm and fuzzy teachers are team players, and the school can depend on them to get things done. At times, everything works out, and their classrooms become a nice place for students to learn and socialize. This level of harmony is the goal of the warm and fuzzy teacher—a goal the burned-out teacher has lost sight of. Toxic and burned-out teachers will avoid warm and fuzzy teachers.

These teachers put much stock into relationship building and find teaching as the ultimate venue for building more relationships. They want to be trusted.

Collaborative Culture

A collaborative culture should be the aim for any school or classroom. When teachers and students share and learn together, the knowledge of one to becomes the knowledge of all. A collaborative teacher is the one other teachers go to when things at school become uncertain or challenging. These teachers can work alone and value autonomy, but they are also aware of times when teams should be built or used to solve a problem.

Teachers who embrace a collaborative culture are aware of the impact of working in teams and how many external factors influence the quality of education each student receives, especially the impact other teachers have on the success of educating the whole student. These teachers are aware of how their own personalities are the greatest influence on the classroom and student success. There is a strong mutual trust built with and among students, so students overlook these teachers' minor mistakes, or the mistakes can be sources of mutual levity.

Collaborative teachers have a collective sense of responsibility toward ensuring students get the best experiences at and away from school. They view collaboration as the best currency for their professional development. They thrive when working in teams and are often cutting-edge teachers who have little patience for weaker teachers who refuse to improve. Collaborative teachers find something special about each class that makes their job worth all the temporary frustrations most teachers experience. They do not point fingers; nor do they indict other adults in the building when students complain.

Classroom activities infuse authentic, active student engagement. Students enjoy the structure as well as the autonomy they receive. Students know other effective teachers respect this teacher.

Collaborative teachers enjoy interactions with the principal, hoping to gain new insights into teaching and learning, inviting the principal to check out new methods or potential problems. The principal learns a lot from these teachers and may use them as examples. Whenever collaborative teachers share their ideas with colleagues, they try to make their ideas feel like gentle refinements of the past, rather than indictments of incompetence. They are risk takers with a healthy dose of skepticism. Any charismatic qualities that emerge do not supplant their acknowledgement of areas for continued growth. Collaborative teachers can seem slow to react, as they call time-out for a meeting so they can collaborate on solutions to problems. They will stand up to and resist toxic teachers.

These teachers have had enough positive experiences in schools to outweigh any type of negativity that might erupt. They have seen the power of collaboration and have learned when best to use it.

Organic Culture

Some might call teachers who embrace an organic culture as back-to-nature people. They have a Zen quality about them that can cause classroom experiences to transcend the specified curriculum. To these teachers, allowing students to express themselves is more important than any other aspect of the curriculum. Organic teachers occasionally take the class outside to work in a natural setting. They feel comfortable taking class time to let students discuss their personal problems and will use that information to make the curriculum relevant. These teachers expend a lot of energy to get struggling or challenging students to trust them, as these teachers understand the power of mentoring. Struggling students seem to do well in this classroom culture and often seek the organic teacher's personal opinions about life, even away from the classroom.

His or her identification with challenging students leads to few behavioral issues in the classroom, but when misbehavior does occur, the teacher feels a sense of disloyalty and is hurt more than what other teachers might experience given the same situation.

Organic teachers enjoy trying new methods or projects at the expense of not completing old ones. The principal may consider these teachers effective since they provide an oasis for the discipline-problem students. These teachers believe the adult world is too serious, so educators should provide opportunities for students to laugh and have a good time. They tend to dress more like students—not so much sloppy as trendy. The principal knows if these teachers cannot reach certain students, nobody can.

The organic teacher has little respect for traditions, finding most obsolete. They have a charismatic quality only certain students perceive. Traditional teachers are often unimpressed with any sense of accomplishment an organic teacher may have; these types of teachers tend to avoid one another. Organic classrooms may seem chaotic at times, but the activity has purpose. The socializing that occurs could make a traditional teacher very uncomfortable, but learning is undeniably happening.

These teachers see everything in a student's world as potential for a new idea or learning opportunity; they see the world as a resource rather than as something to conquer.

Helpless Culture

Helpless teachers create a classroom culture in which students are in control most of the time. The teacher usually lets students talk about whatever they feel is important that day. Students get the teacher off track fairly easily, and at times may waste a whole class period. Helpless teachers occasionally have successes in the classroom, perhaps when they engage students in a discussion or give an assignment that feels relevant to students. More often than not, the class will be somewhat noisy and chaotic, with the same students sent to the office on a regular basis.

Helpless teachers have learned not to share their opinions and, in the light of any criticisms, they back off their beliefs in public. Trust is an important commodity to these teachers, but they find it difficult to build. Their loyalty is with the strongest person, usually (but not always) the principal. They are constantly asking other teachers how they manage to survive and what secrets they might have. They invite colleagues to help them with their personal decisions, often to the point of other teachers avoiding them. When people laugh, these teachers usually assume it is about them and may become defensive. Helpless teachers take it personally if other teachers criticize them in any capacity or offer help without asking first. Perhaps as a way to bring about some sense of loyalty, they will let the principal know (by tattling) which of their colleagues are not supportive of the school. Helpless teachers tend to be high maintenance but hide it with a spurious sense of collaboration.

These teachers typically let other people make decisions for them and may be in the field of education because someone told them to do it.

Toxic Culture

Toxic teachers create classroom cultures that are not conducive for learning in any aspect. These teachers believe that the less students interact with them, the better day they will have. In fact, toxic teachers may even sense more power when students become upset, feel helpless, and avoid them. Despite this, toxic teachers feel students often take advantage of them and can have a victim mentality. They don't think they can trust anyone in the building—and to some degree, not even themselves. Toxic teachers actually consider it a good sign if others think of them as *mean*.

Anytime something goes wrong, toxic teachers are the first to blame new programs, students, parents, other teachers, or the principal. Their best laughs come when new teachers make mistakes, as successful new teachers may make them feel threatened. A goal of toxic teachers is to perpetuate a miserable environment; it is also important to them to try to indoctrinate new teachers into their philosophy of teaching, hoping that few of the newbies will take pride in the school. They enjoy sharing all the past failures of the school with whomever will listen. These conversations may occur in or out of school.

Toxic teachers may be seen as risk takers, since this approach usually finds them in the minority, constantly going against formal leadership while forming a small cadre of their own to do battle. They can be arrogant and condescending, especially to those who choose not to join them. They may have some charismatic qualities but use them to discredit others who are trying to make a difference. Toxic teachers sell their form of obstinacy by using faulty logic. Their classrooms are usually very quiet. Students dislike coming to class, and some may look for ways to get sent to the office or hallway. These teachers apply rules inconsistently, depending on their mood that day or which student they are dealing with. Toxic teachers have little use for the principal and are often most uncomfortable around warm and fuzzy teachers.

Toxic teachers are not the same as negative teachers. Negative teachers still care about the school; they just have poor ways of showing it. Toxic teachers only care about themselves, at any cost to others. These teachers may have once had the potential to become effective teachers but probably lost trust in the system.

Burned-Out Culture

Burnout is a form of survival or coping with something that is frustrating yet inescapable. The worst part of the burned-out teacher's day is pretending he or she likes the job, the school, or even the students. These teachers have forgotten why they became teachers and really dislike the organic, warm and fuzzy, traditional, and collaborative teachers.

Burned-out teachers create classroom cultures that are usually unhappy places until Friday. These teachers can usually tell you how many days are left until the next vacation or holiday and may have a countdown of days left on the board visible to everyone. They consider *student trust* a luxury *other* teachers have that permits students to get away with more and perhaps do less. These teachers may have once been successful but are now tired of trying to be nice. For them, each class could be better if not for a few students. While this may be a common sentiment across many classrooms, burned-out teachers dwell on this notion and often share it openly. They may reduce their classroom workload to assigning and grading worksheets, an everyday activity that simply feels like passing time. Occasionally, they might break the monotony by showing a movie in class that has little to do with the specified curriculum.

Burned-out teachers' relationship with the principal is strained, as they seem to contribute little positivity to the school. They may be easy to replace if they leave for another position, but other schools will likely be hesitant to hire them, so they stay. Burned-out teachers struggle to understand how other teachers believe they can make a difference. They feel like they have given the system their best shot and lost; they now stay in it for the financial security, living for the weekends, and slowly counting down to retirement. These teachers quit caring a long time ago, so they often go about the day in a fog.

Classroom Culture Assessment

Teachers need to understand what their ideal classroom culture might look like compared to their current classroom. To help facilitate this process, we created the chart in figure 4.2 (page 68) to help you better understand and assess the type of culture you have in your classroom. Reflecting on this chart should provide you with a new perspective and vocabulary to assess and identify the type of social environment you create for learning. These descriptions should help assist you with interpretation and reflection.

In addition, this activity is designed to help you understand the type of predominant teacher or classroom culture you may exhibit to the school, given identified behaviors and beliefs. Each row in the chart is built from constructs at the classroom level. We chose not to utilize the specific elements of culture mentioned in previous chapters, as these constructs provide additional themes to consider. These rows provide a means for looking at yourself and your classroom practices through themes of culture at the classroom level. Once you identify where you are in relation to the other cultures, you may choose to change.

The following provides an explanation of each row in figure 4.2.

- **Communication:** The degree to which students receive information (one way or two way) determines much of the culture. Also, the degree to which the teacher allows students to respond—formally or informally—is crucial. "Teachers and students communicate with one another within the temporal, spatial, normative, and material boundaries of the classroom. How [teachers] organize that communication greatly determines the learning which takes place in school" (Florio-Ruane, 2001, p. 10).

- **Trust:** Trust is critical for any group of people that intends on working together. It evolves over time and works best through cooperative opportunities. Trust in a classroom builds when students and the teacher openly share personal opinions and information, encourage one another, and eliminate verbal and nonverbal put-downs (Bryk & Schneider, 2002).

- **Climate:** Climate is a big indicator of the way people feel about how things are going (Sergiovanni, 2001). Their perceptions become reality. Students' comfort levels will influence their willingness to learn. The classroom climate is the collective perceptions of students and the teacher. The teacher may find time to show a personal interest in students and build good rapport with them in order to create a desirable climate, or may discount or ignore issues. Climate can also vary from day to day or even hour to hour.

- **Student chemistry:** Student chemistry is about the makeup of the class and how a particular group of students contributes to the effectiveness of the whole setting and instructional process. This dimension also looks at the degree to which the teacher perceives the current group's potential. Here, teacher expectations play a big role in determining student success. A teacher's first-period class may be different from his or her fifth-period class simply because of student chemistry.

- **Pedagogy:** This element of classroom culture is about the delivery of instruction or philosophical approach to teaching. Teachers may utilize a single approach or experiment with a variety of approaches. Pedagogy is

Directions: Assign ten points to each row, putting the most points in the cells that best describe you or your beliefs. Be open and honest in your responses. There may be qualities in each cell that could describe what you do or believe. The challenge is to determine which is most "you," and give those the most points. Be sure your total for each row equals ten. Column totals should help determine which of the types best describes who you are as a teacher—meaning, the type of classroom culture you tend to establish. Try to do this activity on a normal day, not one that might be wrought with high or low emotions.

Communication	I should keep student talking to a minimum. Points: ___	I keep my personal life out of the classroom. Points: ___	The needy students usually determine what I talk about with this class. Points: ___	Sometimes the students and I take time in class to talk about our personal lives. Points: ___	I let students discuss their personal problems with me. Points: ___	I have learned not to have an opinion about anything around here. Points: ___	The less students talk, the better day I will have. Points: ___	I don't want to accept any happiness until Friday. Points: ___
Trust	As a teacher, I deserve unconditional student respect. Points: ___	I do not need anyone to trust me to be successful. Points: ___	I will use many types of rewards to improve student attitudes. Points: ___	I have developed a strong mutual trust with most students. Points: ___	I expend a lot of energy to get the "bad" students to trust me. Points: ___	I hope students trust me. Points: ___	I don't think I can trust anyone in this building. Points: ___	If I have students' trust, this job is easier to tolerate. Points: ___
Climate	How people feel has little to do with their ability to teach or learn. Points: ___	How students feel about this school does not impact my success. Points: ___	As a teacher, I should make students feel good. Points: ___	How I feel about being at this school determines how effective I am. Points: ___	Allowing students to express themselves is the most important part of school. Points: ___	I usually let students talk about whatever they feel is important that day. Points: ___	I feel more powerful when I make students upset. Points: ___	I am tired of trying to be a nice person. Points: ___
Student Chemistry	Whether students like me or not will not change what I do. Points: ___	Eventually I figure out what works on my own. Points: ___	I need students to like me. Points: ___	There is something special about each class that makes this job worth doing. Points: ___	Students with problems seek my personal opinion about many things. Points: ___	I am constantly asking other teachers how they manage to survive. Points: ___	I often feel that students take advantage of me. Points: ___	If not for a few students, I could tolerate this class. Points: ___
Pedagogy	I grade on a curve. Points: ___	How I teach is nobody's business. Points: ___	I don't like pushing students out of their comfort zones. Points: ___	I try to design active engagement in all my classes. Points: ___	It seems like I am always trying new projects at the expense of not completing old ones. Points: ___	Students can get me off track fairly easily. Points: ___	I am perceived as a "mean" teacher, which is a good thing. Points: ___	It is difficult assigning and grading homework every day. Points: ___

Principal's Role	The principal should keep law and order so I can teach. Points: ___	As long as I continue to do well, I think the principal will leave me alone. Points: ___	I support everything the principal wants to do, and I encourage others to also. Points: ___	I enjoy interactions with the principal. Points: ___	The principal appreciates me helping students who get into trouble. Points: ___	I involve the principal in many decisions I make throughout the day. Points: ___	Usually when something goes wrong in the school, it is the principal's fault. Points: ___	Principals don't remember how difficult it is to teach. Points: ___
Humor	Students laughing in class is usually a sign of off-task behavior. Points: ___	I can use humor in my room if it seems to motivate students. Points: ___	Students will not learn unless they are happy. Points: ___	I enjoy laughing with students. Points: ___	I encourage students to laugh and have a good time. Points: ___	When people laugh, I usually assume it is about me. Points: ___	My best laughs come when new teachers make mistakes. Points: ___	Sometimes I have the class watch a fun movie just to get through the week. Points: ___
Other Teachers	Veteran teachers are usually the best teachers. Points: ___	I have a life separate from other teachers. Points: ___	I like to bring food for other teachers to keep the peace. Points: ___	I draw energy from collaborating with other teachers. Points: ___	I wish teachers would ask me how to help students with problems. Points: ___	I take it personally if other teachers criticize me in any capacity. Points: ___	I am a great teacher, and I don't need any help. Points: ___	I don't understand how teachers feel like they can make a difference. Points: ___
Tradition	This school will never be as good as it once was. Points: ___	Traditions don't bother me as long as I can still do my own thing. Points: ___	I should not change anything if it prevents people from becoming upset. Points: ___	Improvements should feel like gentle refinements of the past. Points: ___	Many of our school traditions seem silly. Points: ___	I let the principal know which teachers do not support school traditions. Points: ___	I enjoy sharing all the past failures of this school. Points: ___	A difficult part of this job is pretending like our school traditions mean something. Points: ___
	Traditional	Independent	Warm and Fuzzy	Collaborative	Organic	Helpless	Toxic	Burned Out
	Total ___	Total ___	Total ___	Total ___	Total ___	Total ___	Total ___	Total ___

Figure 4.2: Classroom culture assessment.

Visit go.SolutionTree.com/schoolimprovement for a free reproducible version of this figure.

the link between the curriculum and assessment. Teachers may choose to be flexible in their delivery, differentiating for individual students, or they may be fairly rigid, putting most of the onus on students to learn. How a teacher teaches is a very personal thing and can be the most difficult to change (Wagner, 2000).

- **Principal's role:** This dimension looks at the degree to which the principal influences teacher behavior and classroom performance. Principals, and the structures that encompass building leadership, may provide some parameters for teachers in their expression of an effective classroom (Sergiovanni, 2001), as well as the degree to which teachers value improvement.

- **Humor:** Literature on learning presents a strong case for the infusion of humor as a means for improving student engagement. Humor taps into emotions, which creates links when learning (Banas, Dunbar, Rodriguez, & Liu, 2011). These teachers have the capacity to see how finding humor, even in their own actions and mistakes, can build student trust.

- **Other teachers:** Other teachers will collectively build the expectations, norms, and values of new faculty. The building culture influences the type of culture that evolves in each classroom. And how the rest of the faculty responds to a teacher's behavior will shape that teacher's future performances. Faculty peer pressure is stronger than any other influence in a teacher's profession (Lortie, 1975; Rosenholtz, 1991). Veteran teachers most influence new teachers (Whitaker, 2010).

- **Tradition:** The accumulation of customs, rituals, and ceremonies provide a peek into the past—those things schools and teachers valued for many years. Some traditions retain their value, while others become obsolete. Determining whether a tradition still serves a purpose can be a source of conflict or pride. In fact, teachers perform many rituals without question, even when they have lost their educational purpose other than preserving the past (Deal & Peterson, 1999; Sarason, 1996).

Through self-assessment, teachers may discover a predominant pattern, thus categorizing themselves within the typology that best describes their classroom and themselves. The typology does not claim that any one type will perfectly fit the patterns of any one teacher or classroom. Rather, many teachers may find themselves within two or more cultural types, though one type should predominate. Additionally, secondary teachers may feel that some of their classes have a certain type of culture, while others may lean a different way. Elementary teachers may feel that before lunch, they have one culture and after lunch, they have another. These are probably more climate than culture, but the feelings can be very real.

Imagine a teacher who completes the classroom culture activity and discovers he or she is maintaining a predominantly traditional classroom. Given the preceding information about traditional cultures, it may not be the best setting relative to a collaborative classroom culture. What happens next? In some schools, teachers either deny the data as accurate or provide evidence that a traditional classroom can be effective in the school. There are many ways for teachers to justify their classroom cultures. In fact, the school culture will be the first to tell anyone that what they are doing now is and has always been OK. The culture determines what is acceptable despite what any policy or research might state.

In some schools, leaders will encourage teachers to reflect on these data, share them with others, and build plans to transform their classrooms into more effective settings, that is, have more traits of collaborative settings and less traits of traditional, burned-out, helpless, or toxic settings. It won't always be a wholesale change, and it will not happen quickly. It can't happen quickly, and preferably it doesn't, because any organization set up to accommodate quick change will be vulnerable to quick, negative changes as well.

To improve teacher effectiveness, leaders should allow teachers to self-administer the classroom culture assessment in figure 4.2 (page 68) and then encourage them to share their findings with other teachers they trust and who are also (and this is important) the most effective in the building (Whitaker, 2010). Leaders should help teachers experience some small wins in the near future to help them build some grit for when the bigger changes later on create more challenges. A small win is equal to making a small change, perhaps one that few will notice, and work from there to take on bigger changes.

The types of classroom cultures in figure 4.1 (page 59) and figure 4.2 also can be conceptualized with a wheel, as shown in figure 4.3 (page 72). This model helps illustrate how the types of classroom cultures are juxtaposed. There are polar opposites, which supports the idea that some teachers are unaware of, indifferent to, or in direct conflict with other teachers. Cultures directly across from each other usually have teachers that do not enjoy each other's company—their approach to teaching may be in conflict, as well as their attitude toward students in general, which can often lead to an argument. Those closer to each other on the wheel may have teachers who share some aspects of their approach to education and are friendly to each

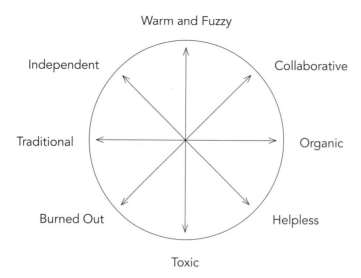

Figure 4.3: Classroom culture typology wheel.

other. This image might help you imagine or visualize how a social network might develop in a school, and explain why certain teachers seem to gravitate toward, or avoid, other teachers.

Each classroom will have a unique feel to it. When educators walk into a classroom, they can sense a strong level of caring, rigor, and inclusiveness, or a noticeable lack of these qualities (Buchanan-Rivera, 2017). Much of what classroom visitors feel is a reflection of the teacher's personality. If the teacher cares, the classroom will promote that affect through various elements (such as climate and routines) in organizational culture (Gruenert & Whitaker, 2015). Since the classroom culture is an extension of the teacher, it then becomes a challenge for any teacher to change it.

Teachers will have limits in any given school. They cannot become too good or too bad (too fast) and still retain their assigned role. As school leaders consider the restraints the school's culture imposes on those who want to improve, leaders should be aware of those restraints, identify them, and begin conversations regarding removing these restraints. If Ms. Smith wants to become a better teacher, what does that mean, and what does it look like? Who is planning on stopping her? Who might want to support her or help her get there?

The classroom climate is one of many elements that help define a classroom. Other elements converge with the climate to bring a unique experience to students in that classroom. Over time, some teachers may feel stuck in the culture or by their role; some will thrive and choose to stay regardless of pay, as they sense the intrinsic value of mastering teaching. This dynamic is what attracts educators to the field; they receive autonomy to create their own classrooms or permission to create a learning space that they think works best. Most teachers bring their best, hoping to make students' experiences very meaningful.

A few teachers, however, might not try to maximize their potential. State and district curricula, grade-level and subject mandates, and so on, might make teachers feel restricted, but the climate and culture are still dramatically different among teachers in a school. The teacher is still by far the most significant factor in the classroom and everyone in the room knows it. Remember, cultures do not emerge quickly. It takes many weeks, months, or even years for a true culture to evolve into a force strong enough to have a significant impact. If teachers want to change students' attitudes, they must first address their own attitudes.

The classroom culture typology we described previously provides a range of possibilities across a population of teachers in a school. The typology demonstrates the various types of classroom cultures that may exist (allowing for hybrids), so teachers can judge their own efforts and possibly make changes toward becoming more effective educators. The school culture is built around classroom cultures, and classroom cultures get permission from the school's culture, so each classroom will eventually fill a role in the overall school culture.

The school community knows who the fun teachers are, who the "mean" teachers are, who cares about students, who focuses more on athletics, who gives worksheets, who yells, and so on. This predictability among classrooms provides a peek into the school culture's strength—*strength* here meaning level of influence. Some of the less effective classroom settings may struggle to change simply because the school culture won't let them. Some teachers might say, "It's simply who we are around here; we take the good with the bad." And yet, the differences from classroom to classroom in every school are quite dramatic. The more effective the teachers are, the more they know that change and improvement is possible and usually up to them.

Classroom Culture Change

Understanding the degree to which the teacher trusts other teachers impacts the first step in changing his or her classroom culture. The best professional development may be from a colleague down the hall; professional development tends to have the greatest impact in informal settings. In other words, having lunch with another teacher could have more impact than a professional development seminar. Conversations about improving teacher effectiveness are very sensitive, and they should not be treated the same way as delivering a new lunch or bus duty schedule. These conversations can be effective even in a negative school culture. That means change is possible in your setting, using your resources and leadership to make a difference.

Take caution if things are moving too fast, or if it feels too easy, because surface-level impact will be short lived. You might start the change with small, surface-level things, such as rearranging furniture or inviting other teachers in to co-teach a project. Some teachers may get stuck here. To change the classroom culture goes beyond putting up motivational posters and giving high fives as students enter the room. However, do not discount these climate-changing attempts to improve a classroom. Just like changing a culture schoolwide, many times the first step involves improving the climate—a convergence of organizational elements toward new norms and expectations. For this to work, student buy-in is critical. Students must not sense this change is fake or temporary. Just like when principals attempt to make changes at the building level, teachers can sense temporary or fake changes. Making changes with infidelity at the start makes the next effort more difficult (Godin, 2012).

What does all this mean to a teacher? *Practitioners want relevance.* School culture is a hot topic that isn't going away, but some educators might argue whether classroom culture actually exists at all. The classic literature on organizational culture says it takes about three to five years to change any (school) culture (Deal & Peterson, 1990; Fullan & Hargreaves, 1996; Rosenholtz, 1991; Schein, 1992). Teachers might argue that a social setting does not have a culture (or become one) until it has had a few years to mature.

You might wonder how much external forces might impact both the classroom environment and the teaching that happens there. As it turns out, most external forces have little to no impact on the school or classroom culture (Gruenert & Whitaker, 2017). The classroom culture is a product of the teacher's personality and ability, his or her thinking, as well as what other teachers are doing, not so much what the community or parents do.

Imagine if you gave a teacher $10,000 to create the classroom of his or her dreams. Most teachers would be thrilled to have this opportunity. Now imagine giving the same teacher only $50 to do the same thing. In both cases, the same culture will emerge. If a teacher values displaying student work, the teacher with more funding may purchase an elaborate display case, while the teacher with less funding may simply purchase thumb tacks and a corkboard. Two ways to display student work, and two ways to display the same teacher value. The culture did not change with more funding. The way a teacher physically structures his or her classroom—the furniture, lighting, décor, and equipment or supplies placement—indicates the type of culture that exists, not necessarily how much money the teacher spends (Buchanan-Rivera, 2017).

Regardless of any external forces, the teacher makes the culture, and that is the primary driving force of what happens in the classroom. Everything you see in the classroom or watch the teacher do are *artifacts* or *footprints* of a personality that tells you what is important to that person. If you could magically transport all the teachers of one building into a building that was newer, with better equipment, fresh paint, flowers, posters, and so on, each teacher would teach the same way he or she did in the old setting. Yes, the first few weeks may be novel, but as time passes, each teacher settles into that "comfortable place" from before.

Conclusion

The classroom culture typology in this chapter presents a conceptual look at eight possible classroom cultures—representing the beliefs and preferences of the teachers in those classrooms. Knowing what type of classroom culture a teacher creates helps you further understand the values and beliefs of each teacher, as well as identify which teachers might serve as support for those seeking to improve or which teachers might not serve well as mentors to new faculty. We imagine all classrooms will have some traits of each type (except for the toxic classroom culture, which is probably not as prominent as the others), with one type serving as a base from which many behaviors are supported.

You cannot reduce the social architecture of any organization to an exact scale, nor can you build systematic recipes to address a systemic issue (Stalbaum, 2021). Reflecting on the information in this chapter will hopefully reveal some latent issues that may be inhibiting teachers from improving, and it may reveal gifts some teachers can bring to the whole faculty. Identifying these issues and gifts in your school provides an opportunity for everyone to learn.

CHAPTER 5

The Culture Scorecard

In this chapter, we use the concept of a culture scorecard to explain the idea of culture. Our hypothesis is that people tend to "score" many things in their lives, without realizing they do it. The culture scorecard offers people a way to keep score of the things that matter most and also the things that grab their attention.

First, we explain why people tend to score symbols (proxies for values) that organizations produce and brandish rather than actual values or beliefs. Then we provide a culture scorecard you can use to get a deeper understanding of how cultures are formed through an examination of personal traits and values. Finally, we discuss the concept of a classroom scorecard, examining a way to better understand what school culture is, what classroom culture is, and how one might influence the other.

Three Levels of Culture

Schein (2017) theorizes three levels of culture: (1) symbols, (2) espoused values, and (3) assumptions (beliefs). The three levels refer to the degree to which the different cultural phenomena are visible to the observer. Schein (2017) claims that groups choose symbols to support their values and beliefs at deeper levels. You can trace whatever people do or display back to the values they hold. Symbols gain the attention of others, just like a bright light or loud noise.

- *Symbols* are visible elements, such as a logo or mascot, clothing, or paint colors in the hallways, that give us information about a group. For example, if someone wears a Chicago Cubs T-shirt, it is probably because he or she is a fan of the Chicago Cubs and wants others to see that.

- The next level of culture is *espoused values*. Values attract people, causing them to want to learn more about and maybe join a group.

- The deepest level is composed of *assumptions* (beliefs), which are the bedrock of the group. In other words, symbols get peoples' attention, espoused values get them in the door, and beliefs keep them there.

This chapter looks at the symbols that groups produce to attract people to their cause or convince them to buy into their cultural norms. A different way to look at the uniqueness of a group or members of a culture might be to think of its symbols as items on a scorecard. A scorecard measures the things we can see, hear, taste, smell, and feel. It would be difficult to measure someone's values, beliefs, or assumptions. We can see someone wearing a St. Louis Cardinals shirt and usually score that person as a fan of the Cardinals. We cannot look into a person's mind and determine what he or she values, so we assume the value exists by looking at what they outwardly display.

Introductions Scorecard

The scorecard concept is one way of helping people better understand what seems to matter most to them, whether they are aware of it or not. Most values are learned. Teachers learn what is most important to a school through the various manifestations of cultural elements. The scorecard attempts to reveal the things people tend to score in their minds or determine the value of when they are in the company of others—things they learn from the school's culture. Obviously, the terms *mindset, prejudice,* and *bias* are in play. Judging or scoring people on these items can reveal unconscious biases and prejudices people hold that they might not even be aware of. According to Gleb Tsipursky (2020):

> Unconscious bias (also known as implicit bias) refers to unconscious forms of dis-crimination and stereotyping based on race, gender, sexuality, ethnicity, ability, age, and so on. It differs from cognitive bias, which is a predictable pattern of mental errors that result in us misperceiving reality and, as a result, deviating away from the most likely way of reaching our goals.

The scorecard might shed some light on some things that matter, but *should not* matter, and that working in a certain school might discourage, or even encourage. Completing the introductions scorecard might make you aware of some unconscious biases you or your school might hold.

Consider completing the introductions scorecard in figure 5.1 the next time you are introduced to a new group (for example, a new class of students, new faculty, or a new committee). Rather than doing the typical introductions (asking group members to state their names and what they did last summer), ask them to complete the

Personal Traits	Positive Points 1 2 3 4 5 Doesn't Matter = 0	Negative Points –1 –2 –3 –4 –5 Doesn't Matter = 0	Total Points
New or veteran teacher			
Subject taught			
Friend of administrators			
Athletic coach			
Clothes worn			
University graduated from			
Military experience			
Educational goals			
Tone and vocabulary			
Physical stature			
Engagement in class			
Married or parents			

Figure 5.1: Introductions scorecard.

*Visit **go.SolutionTree.com/schoolimprovement** for a free reproducible version of this figure.*

introductions scorecard. Whether you ask them to or not, group members are going over similar questions and reflections in their minds (new or veteran teacher, subject taught, educational goals, and so on, of everyone else in the room). People do it all the time. You can use the scorecard concept to create a rubric that best represents what people value or search for in your school. In your mind, which of these traits matters most? Note that some toxic school teachers or cultures might actually judge people based on race, gender, (dis)ability, and so on. Not only is it wrong to judge people based on these factors, it is illegal. People in these groups are protected under U.S. and Canadian law (for more information, see the U.S. Equal Employment Opportunity Commission website: www.eeoc.gov, and the Justice Laws website, Employment Equity Act: https://laws-lois.justice.gc.ca/eng/acts/E-5.401/page-1.html).

In most situations, when strangers come together, the group leader will introduce him- or herself. The leader then orchestrates the introductions for everyone else.

This is one way of breaking the ice among people so a climate of trust can begin to develop. While this all likely works fine, there is something else happening underneath.

Sometimes it seems that life is a contest. The person who "has the most" generally rises in status among the others; the definition of *most* depends on what the group values. In some social or occupational groups, people sometimes find one-upmanship taking place as introductions become a resume contest.

While most introductions may only last a few seconds, some people will share their "personal scars" whenever they get the chance. This may cause an informal social hierarchy to evolve that can be difficult to avoid, even in the most professional settings. It also causes informal cliques to start cropping up. People like the people they share commonalities with, and they use introductions to search for that crucial common ground. People also want to be with people who make them look better. They pay special attention to who they see and what they hear to determine who they can trust. This is the culture at work. Though this may seem like something children do, adults are just as prone to it. Introductions tend to build first impressions, and these impressions of others create an anchor people use to confirm what they first believed (Schein, 2009).

When introducing themselves, some may be able finish in a few seconds, while others may spend too much time self-validating. You may spin your introduction to best meet group expectations—creating a persona that aligns well with those expectations—even if it means drifting a bit from reality. We call it *rounding up*. Is it possible for trust to evolve more quickly without introductions or hierarchy? Can you make it more personal without getting too personal?

Figure 5.2 shows twelve traits that the members of three different school cultures have ranked from 1–10 according to what is most important to them. A 1 denotes the most important trait. The higher numbers are important, but not as much as number 1. Don't assume a trait ranked a 10 is weak or irrelevant; it is still a value held by the group that helps identify what group members think are important. Remember, these are things we see as we are introduced as well as things we may learn about people as they introduce themselves.

Some cultures may have other traits that truly matter. Figure 5.2 is just an example of a comparison of three cultures. In culture 1, the experience of the teacher is most important. Perhaps when interviewing, the search committee might place value on experience and assume a veteran teacher will bring more to the table. In some schools, however, the search committee might assume that experience equates to the candidate being stuck in his or her ways. In culture 2, educational goals are most valued; and in culture 3, the most important trait is military experience.

Personal Traits	Culture 1	Culture 2	Culture 3
New or veteran teacher	1	10	8
Subject taught	12	5	7
Friend of administrators	5	11	10
Athletic coach	2	6	6
Clothes worn	8	14	2
University graduated from	13	7	11
Educational goals	10	1	9
Military experience	11	12	1
Tone and vocabulary	6	8	13
Physical stature	14	9	5
Engagement in class	3	3	14
Married or parent	9	4	4

Figure 5.2: Personal traits scorecard.

Culture has a big voice in how to evaluate people. Chances are, the members of a long-standing group will have a culture that has assimilated their thinking on a few things, and their scorecards will have strong similarities.

The culture whispers in people's ears regarding what is most important—or how to rank these items. As a school leader, bringing this to light makes a dent in the power of a culture, as it can no longer hide. If you share with the group what type of scorecard the school has, it takes away some of the power the culture has, but it also puts you in a precarious position. It can make you seem like a nonmember, being critical of what the group values.

In a scene from the movie *A Few Good Men* (Reiner, Brown, & Scheinman, 1992), a marine states his priorities as *unit, corps, God, country*—his own scorecard that he learned from the group he values most—the marine corps. We then assume that all marines will adopt these values, in this order, to be accepted and successful. Marines live by this code, and it expresses loyalty and honor. If you were to visit other organizations (such as hospitals, churches, or football teams), you might find different values that matter most. In schools, the list may be different across one district with many schools, perhaps sharing a few values, but probably not in the same order. Each school will have its own scorecard that new teachers quickly learn and use as a means for becoming part of the group.

Author and educator Tony Wagner (2000) shares how positive schools will have the following traits: (1) core values, (2) caring, and (3) collaboration. Imagine the symbols a positive school might display given these traits. What would you see to support these traits? In a negative school, you might find selfishness and territoriality rather than caring. Moreover, a negative school might value competition rather than collaboration. Imagine how a school might symbolize these beliefs. Symbols support all beliefs that become items on the scorecard, which in turn become symbols of what matters most. Wagner (2000) claims that in a positive school, *core values* are the road the organization travels on, *caring* is the attitude of the travelers, and *collaboration* is the means by which they move.

An ex-athlete may want *sports prowess* to be most important. Someone who married a lawyer or doctor might want this status to carry the most sway. Is there a way to have this significance be based on the most effective teacher in a school? Would that change the culture in your building? What if you put *great teaching* on the school scorecard? How would it be scored? We think this could have many implications for the recruitment and retention of new, effective teachers. If you feel the scoring of the items that should matter most don't actually matter most, then items on the scorecard will need to change.

Questions you need to consider when changing a scorecard include the following.

- How do items get on a scorecard?
- How do you remove items?
- What happens when you share your new scorecard?
- Who might not want anything to change?

Classroom Scorecard

If there are scorecards wherever people tend to gather or judge others, then a classroom scorecard is as valuable as a schoolwide scorecard. This activity is simply another way for educators to better understand what school culture is, what classroom culture is, and maybe how to change or improve them. Much like how the school culture impacts the classroom culture, the school's scorecard will have some influence on the classroom scorecard. Again, your scorecard shows what is important to you. It is what you use to form first impressions about other people, especially at first meetings.

In the classroom, the teacher's scorecard sets the tone for the class and makes it a place students want to be—or not. A teacher's classroom scorecard may be limited in how much it can change. Once a school establishes the role the teachers play in that school, it can be set in stone.

When building a classroom scorecard, what might be most important to a teacher regarding what happens in the classroom? Following are a few elements he or she might consider.

- Cleanliness
- Rules
- Aesthetics

- Safety
- Student work
- Personal touches

- Cultural awareness
- Teaching methods

Leaders could use these elements to compare and contrast the scorecards of a positive classroom and a negative classroom. Each of these elements will manifest in different ways, depending on the values and beliefs of the teacher. And most teachers will find the school's culture (or scorecard) to be very influential in what appears on their classroom scorecards. Figure 5.3 (page 84) provides a template for comparing and contrasting the characteristics of an effective, positive classroom with a classroom that is typically ineffective and negative.

Think about when you enter a classroom and notice these traits or characteristics. Think of them as items on a scorecard, not an evaluation, and more important, how they became that way. When scoring, use a scale from –5 to 5. The positive numbers tell us the degree to which a trait is valued, while the negative numbers suggest the trait is more than *not* valued, it is despised. For example, one teacher might have an ultra-clean classroom with stringent rules about dropping paper on the floor, while the teacher next door might not see paper on the floor as an issue and finds notes from the custodian insulting. Scoring the item as a zero means the trait is not important. Provide a brief description of the trait in each cell that you score.

From a systems perspective, you could assert that all the traits in figure 5.3 interrelate, meaning most will have a root cause or value in that setting. The teacher creates a classroom based on his or her values and beliefs, typically coming from life experiences as well as school values. To quickly blame an ineffective teacher for a negative classroom culture is dismissing the power of the school's cultural influence, which is a reflection of the school's leadership.

As you look at your scores in this activity, consider the strong issues, those with scores above a positive 2 or below a negative 2. These traits may be extremes that

Classroom Traits	Positive and Effective 5 4 3 2 1 0	Negative and Ineffective –5 –4 –3 –2 –1 0
Cleanliness	Description: Score:	Description: Score:
Rules	Description: Score:	Description: Score:
Aesthetics	Description: Score:	Description: Score:
Safety	Description: Score:	Description: Score:
Student work	Description: Score:	Description: Score:
Personal touches	Description: Score:	Description: Score:
Cultural awareness	Description: Score:	Description: Score:
Teaching methods	Description: Score:	Description: Score:

Figure 5.3: Comparing and contrasting classroom scorecards.

*Visit **go.SolutionTree.com/schoolimprovement** for a free reproducible version of this figure.*

make your classroom unique. Being unique is not always a good thing. Can a teacher be so concerned with cleanliness that a daily ritual of cleaning becomes an annoying ceremony? Can a teacher personalize a classroom with so many cartoon character images as to be distracting?

Again, we are trying to make the subtle nuances of what happens in classrooms more obvious by making it empirical and observable—revealing the things we do in the classroom that might not be effective. The goal is not to make any teacher feel bad, rather, we hope to shed light on more of what is happening, and how the classroom climate could shift to a better setting with a few small changes.

Conclusion

We may not be able to get teachers to stop scoring the people they encounter, but we might be able to modify their scorecards. Knowing how a desired trait gets on or off a scorecard is knowing how a culture can be changed or improved. The classroom scorecard will be somewhat bound to the school scorecard, depending on the strength of the school culture. Comparing scorecards might help some teachers understand the types of classroom cultures they have relative to the ones they want, and who might have the classroom culture they want to visit and observe. As in any type of culture change or improvement effort, start small with inconspicuous change and work on the bigger changes from there. The culture is ready to stop any changes, so we will need to sneak in the side door.

CHAPTER 6

The Capacity to Change

In this chapter, we ask school leaders to determine if their schools have the capacity to change before they actually introduce any type of change. There is typically discomfort with any change, even changes for the better. The climate of the school is, in many ways, a measure of staff satisfaction and happiness. When the discomfort of a needed change comes, is it the job of school leaders to ensure nobody is uncomfortable? Nobody signs a teaching contract that states happiness will be maintained or positive satisfaction levels will remain constant. If staff in a school feel unhappy for a long enough period of time, then unhappiness becomes the *new normal*, and soon, the culture will redefine *happiness* so the culture does not have to change. New teachers will learn what it means to be happy as quickly as they learn to fit in, or they will leave.

Having the capacity to change means being able to do what is best for the school. It is essential for leaders to understand that everyone is not the same. Sounds simple, but satisfying a very negative person might be either impossible or come at the cost of more productive staff members' satisfaction. If a negative teacher is always complaining, a principal moving students from his or her class to a more effective teacher's class may help the negative teacher, but it will not be a positive result for the teacher who now has more students in his or her class. Understanding the satisfaction of the whole group is important, but leaders must ensure they do not damage more productive contributors in order to pacify people who cannot be satisfied. Moving the students to a new class probably didn't improve the negative teacher's attitude at all, and it could possibly reinforce complaining as the tool for any teacher to get his or her own way in the school. This change was not what was best for the school; perhaps it happened because the principal did not think other changes were possible.

Before cultural change can begin, school leaders must assess how prepared their staff are for change. In previous chapters, we discuss the difficulty of changing cultures in schools and the importance of knowing the difference between climate change and culture change. In this chapter, we try to help visualize a staff's capacity to change a culture using a new theory. While some of this theory may initially seem complex, it's ultimately a simple solution to a multifaceted issue. This chapter also examines the speed of culture change and realizing that there are no quick fixes when it comes to culture. Knowing the ins and outs of school culture only matters if the staff are prepared and able to change.

Assumptions Guiding the Theory of Capacity to Change

Remember, everyone is different and as a result, the capacity to change varies greatly between people, even those in the same school. Having a few people willing to experiment with new ideas does not always mean the organization has capacity to change. Not only does the type of change matter, but most of all, it matters who thinks it will work. The informal leaders behind the scenes will become obvious and useful. Let's take a look at some of the assumptions that guide this approach.

1. Real change occurs at the grassroots level (Woodman & Pasmore, 1996).
2. Employees most often change through peer influence (Patterson et al., 2008).
3. Organizational capacity to change is equal to the collective change capacity of its members.
4. Formal leadership can influence an organization's capacity to change (Fullan, 2011).
5. Change is a manifestation of learning something new (Senge et al., 2012).

Real Change Occurs at the Grassroots Level

What teachers do in the classroom—specifically, deliver instruction—is the main target of improvement efforts. The many administrative layers above the teacher can change, but student academic performance will not improve until the teacher changes his or her instruction. The classroom level is the grassroots level.

Employees Most Often Change Through Peer Influence

This assumption is all about the culture of the organization or school. Each school will have opinion leaders—people who may or may not be in official leadership roles but who nevertheless serve as the interpreters of reality. A few people in each school have the ability to influence many others, while many people have the ability to influence a few others. Whatever one's capacity is to change, that is the level of change he or she is "selling" to others throughout day-to-day interactions. Using the theory, those with the greatest selling power or social influence are the key players. It is important to remember that every organization will have a few people who are against *any* change, and they have the ability to sell that perspective if leaders do nothing.

Organizational Capacity to Change Equals the Collective Change Capacity of Its Members

This assumption may be the largest conceptual leap in the theory of capacity to change. Basically, if everyone can do something well, then the whole school has the capacity to do something well. Conversely, if everyone (or perhaps, most everyone) is unable to perform well, then the school will probably not do well (in whatever the task may be). Having capacity does not mean the school is doing a task well, but it has the skills and potential to do the task well. From the perspective of this theory, if all members have the capacity to change, then the school has the capacity to change too. The challenge is when only a portion of the group in a school has this capacity. At what point does the school reach a threshold of having sufficient members in the group with the capacity to permit the school to change?

Within the structure of the theory of capacity to change, leaders must account for those who have the capacity to change, those who have little capacity, and those who have none. They must also consider those who despise change. Imagine a group of ten people; eight are willing to change and two are not. The theory argues this group has more capacity to change than a group of ten with eight unwilling to change and only two who are willing to change. While it may sound like simple mathematics, weight is given to those who can influence others, thus, the mathematics gets complex as leaders account for those with influence having more weight in some decisions. Think of it this way: in a school or district meeting, are there usually certain people who everyone listens to? And are there certain people to whom others automatically react negatively? So, it depends on who are the two and who are the eight.

Formal Leadership Influences Organizational Capacity to Change

No matter the demeanor of those in a school, the attitude of leadership will have a huge impact on the possibilities for change. This is particularly important when it comes to determining capacity to change, as ineffective leaders may force change in situations that demand none, while effective leaders are keenly aware of where they can make a genuine impact.

Change Is a Manifestation of Learning Something New

If change occurs, it is because people in an organization learned something new. For these purposes, the words *learned* and *change* are virtually synonymous. Schools seek to change to improve what they do. For this change to occur, members need to learn something new. Having the capacity to change is basically having the *capacity to learn*. If someone learns a better way to do something, he or she will probably do it. Think of classroom management. If an educator could get students to behave better, he or she would—but until he or she knows *how*, the potential for better student behavior is quite limited.

The Process for Change

Just like individuals do, every organization, or school, has the capacity to change. However, this capacity can vary from person to person and school to school, depending on the established culture and staff willingness and capability. The following process can help you identify the capacity to change in your own school.

1. Determine each individual's capacity to change and level of social influence.
2. Compute a mean score for each person and plot on a graph.
3. Compute a mean score for the school using weights from each individual.

Determine Each Individual's Capacity to Change and Level of Social Influence

The first step in the change process is to determine the following for each individual: (1) capacity to change and (2) level of social influence. While you cannot look into people's minds and measure these traits, you can conduct a self-assessment for these two items using the two assessments in this section. As with any survey, we can argue about the accuracy of the questions and the dependability of people to respond honestly. However, given a large enough sample, these will be taken care of.

The following are some reasons people are willing to change.

- They find the level of innovation captivating.
- They experiment in other parts of their lives.
- They take risks in other parts of their lives.
- They are willing to try others' ideas.
- They are aware that improvement means changing something.

To determine an individual's capacity to change, we put these items in a self-assessment chart (see figure 6.1). The capacity to change has a scale of –5 to 5. This allows for those who despise change to score themselves in the negative. This suggests that having a score of zero indicates having no opinion about change. While a zero does not mean one avoids change, a negative score does.

	–5	–4	–3	–2	–1	0	1	2	3	4	5
I am innovative.											
I like to experiment with new ideas.											
I like to take risks.											
I am willing to try others' ideas.											
I know that improvement requires change.											

Figure 6.1: Assessment for individual capacity to change.

*Visit **go.SolutionTree.com/schoolimprovement** for a free reproducible version of this figure.*

Following are some reasons people are able to exert social influence.

- They acknowledge the role of emotions in getting things done.
- They are visible and accessible, which is important for trust to grow.
- They believe they are persuasive, which establishes efficacy and confidence.
- Others seek their opinions, which builds informal leadership capacity.
- They enjoy being the center of attention and taking the lead when available.

To assess each individual's level of influence, we put these items in a self-assessment chart (see figure 6.2, page 92). The scale ranges from 1 to 10. There is no negative score for these traits; the scale determines how much influence the individual has, as opposed to the previous change scale, which captures which individuals may fight the change. For example, scoring a 1 on the social influence scale does not mean one does not think social influence is important; it simply indicates that he or she is not very socially influential. This scale tries to identify who the opinion leaders are (positive and negative). There is no zero on this scale, as each person has some level of influence.

	1	2	3	4	5	6	7	8	9	10
I am emotional and expressive.										
I interact with many people each day.										
I am persuasive.										
Many people seek my opinions.										
I enjoy being the center of attention.										

Figure 6.2: Assessment for individual social influence.

*Visit **go.SolutionTree.com/schoolimprovement** for a free reproducible version of this figure.*

With any self-assessment, there is the potential for inaccurate responses—this is a limitation of any survey. Sometimes the process of self-assessment can be untrustworthy—in other words, people are afraid to respond truthfully. This can be affected by a teacher's lack of self-confidence, an untrustworthy leader, or a lack of faith that the results will be used to help the school and teachers grow, rather than being used as a punitive hammer. Because of this, we offer an alternative approach to gaining these data. It may be possible for leaders to assess their members on each scale using the help of other trusted individuals who know these people well.

Compute a Mean Score for Each Assessment

Once you have these data, compute a mean score for each assessment. For the individual capacity to change assessment (see figure 6.1, page 91), each group member should have one score, an average of all five responses, ranging from –5 to 5. Similarly, compute a mean score for the individual social influence assessment (see figure 6.2), which is an average of all five responses, ranging from 1 to 10. To move to the second step, you need two numbers per member, a change capacity number and a social influence number.

Use the matrix in figure 6.3 to indicate where each group member lies relative to everyone else. While it might be interesting to try and compare people at this point, it is simply an inventory of the people we have in this school. The dots in each cell represent a person, but we should not know (or publicly identify) who that person is. Place a dot in the appropriate cell for each member. The vertical axis (y) represents the capacity to change mean. The horizontal axis (x) represents the social influence mean.

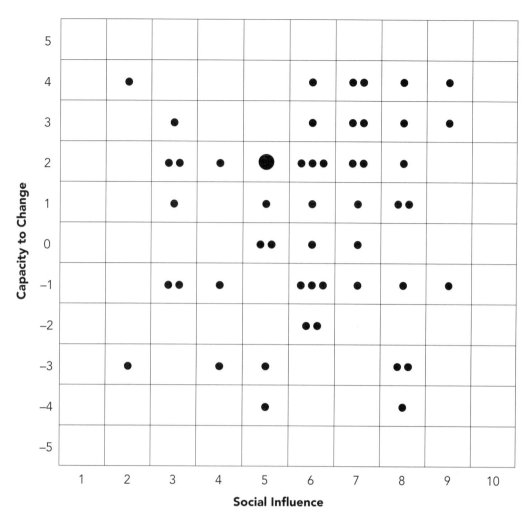

Figure 6.3: Capacity to change matrix example.

*Visit **go.SolutionTree.com/schoolimprovement** for a free blank reproducible version of this figure.*

Each dot represents an individual's location on the matrix according to his or her two numbers—the two means you compute from the capacity to change and social influence assessments (see figure 6.1, page 91, and figure 6.2). If an individual has a mean score of 2 for capacity to change, and a mean score of 5 for social influence, then represent that person with a dot in cells *Y2* and *X5* (that person's dot is larger in figure 6.3. Hang in there; the complex mathematics is about to begin.

Compute a Mean Score for the School Using Weights From Each Individual

Now, we need to compute a mean score for the school using the weights from each individual. Figure 6.3 provides an example of a completed matrix for a group of fifty people. Some cells may contain several dots for people with the same scores, and many cells will remain empty.

After identifying all members according to their capacity to change and their social influence, look at the matrix example in figure 6.3 (page 93). Would you guess this organization has the capacity to change, or does it seem like some members should first work on this capacity? This matrix might convey an idea as to the school's capacity to change, however, there is more mathematics to do.

This is a critical step in assessing your school's capacity to change. A school's capacity to change is not a number based on staff's cumulative capacity, but the degree to which they can sell it (through levels of influence). For example, a person with 10 on influence will outsell five people with 1s (no influence). This helps identify leaders who are whispering in people's ears about whether the school should change.

Figure 6.4 is rather complex, but it shows how to determine the weight for each individual. This is where assumption number three (*organizational capacity to change equals the collective change capacity of its members*) comes in. The number in each cell is an interaction (multiplication) of the capacity to change with social influence. Each person is assigned weight regarding his or her stance on change and the capacity to influence others. For example, if you have a 5 for capacity to change and 10 for social influence, your total is 50 (5 x 10). We changed the 50 to 5 (dividing by 10 to make computations easier), and placed it in the upper-right corner of the matrix.

5	.5	1	1.5	2	2.5	3	3.5	4	4.5	5
4	.4	.8	1.2	1.6	2	2.4	2.8	3.2	3.6	4
3	.3	.6	.9	1.2	1.5	1.8	2.1	2.4	2.7	3
2	.2	.4	.6	.8	1	1.2	1.4	1.6	1.8	2
1	.1	.2	.3	.4	.5	.6	.7	.8	.9	1
0	0	0	0	0	0	0	0	0	0	0
−1	−.1	−.2	−.3	−.4	−.5	−.6	−.7	−.8	−.9	−1
−2	−.2	−.4	−.6	−.8	−1	−1.2	−1.4	−1.6	−1.8	−2
−3	−.3	−.6	−.9	−1.2	−1.5	−1.8	−2.1	−2.4	−2.7	−3
−4	−.4	−.8	−1.2	−1.6	−2	−2.4	−2.8	−3.2	−3.6	−4
−5	−.5	−1	−1.5	−2	−2.5	−3	−3.5	−4	−4.5	−5
	1	2	3	4	5	6	7	8	9	10

Capacity to Change (vertical axis) · Social Influence (horizontal axis)

Figure 6.4: Capacity to change matrix with cell weights example.

Visit go.SolutionTree.com/schoolimprovement for a free blank reproducible version of this figure.

Figure 6.5 provides another example of how you might plot a group's capacity to change, but this time with ten members. This whole-group score represents its capacity to change, as a group.

Capacity to Change	1	2	3	4	5	6	7	8	9	10	Total
5	.5	1	1.5	2	2.5	3	3.5	4	4.5	5	0
4	.4	.8	1.2	1.6	2	2.4	2.8	3.2	3.6	4	.8
3	.3	.6	.9	1.2	1.5	1.8	2.1	2.4	2.7	3	4.2
2	.2	.4	.6	.8	1	1.2	1.4	1.6	1.8	2	2.4
1	.1	.2	.3	.4	.5	.6	.7	.8	.9	1	.5
0	0	0	0	0	0	0	0	0	0	0	0
−1	−.1	−.2	−.3	−.4	−.5	−.6	−.7	−.8	−.9	−1	−.4
−2	−.2	−.4	−.6	−.8	−1	−1.2	−1.4	−1.6	−1.8	−2	−1.4
−3	−.3	−.6	−.9	−1.2	−1.5	−1.8	−2.1	−2.4	−2.7	−3	−2.4
−4	−.4	−.8	−1.2	−1.6	−2	−2.4	−2.8	−3.2	−3.6	−4	0
−5	−.5	−1	−1.5	−2	−2.5	−3	−3.5	−4	−4.5	−5	0

Social Influence

Grand total: 3.7   Divided by 10 = 0.37

Figure 6.5: Capacity to change matrix with scores total per row example.
Visit go.SolutionTree.com/schoolimprovement for a free blank reproducible version of this figure.

To determine the grand total, add up the right column, which when you include all scores, positive and negative, totals 3.7. Since there are ten people in this group, divide that score by 10, which is the final capacity to change score: 0.37.

So far, you know how to use the two scores for each group member to assign him or her a weight. This weight gives you some idea of how much help or hindrance each group member might be when the school faces a potential change. If you have many members who are willing to change and have strong social influence, the theory states that the school is in a better position to change than one with few people willing or many people unwilling who are also influential.

Figure 6.6 (page 96) shows a graphic that places the organizational score in a scale to help determine whether the group is ready for change, or if the leaders need to first invest resources into increasing members' capacity to change.

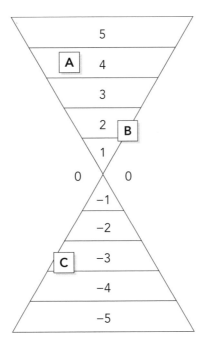

Figure 6.6: Organizational capacity to change graphic example.

Figure 6.6 shows three examples (*A*, *B*, and *C*). The theory says that school A (near a 4.0 score) has a greater chance of experiencing a successful change than either school B (score of around 1.8) or school C (with a score of –3.3). School A has more capacity to change due to the mean of the collective change capacity of its members. Be cautious here—too much capacity to change can result in a group chasing every shiny object they see. School leaders need some degree of discretion when change is an option and not jump on every new idea.

School B has some capacity to change—perhaps a small change could be successful in this setting. School C represents an organization with no capacity to change. In fact, school C has some energy stored up to resist change. The leaders in school C need to get their staff score above *0*, and scale down any changes until the school gets a few easy wins.

One approach to building more capacity for organizational change is to identify who are willing to change and who are the most influential people in the organization. In the book *Influencer*, Patterson and colleagues (2008) refer to these people as *respected and connected*. You can use the capacity to change matrix in figure 6.3 (page 93) to help identify who you might want at the table when discussing and implementing future school-improvement initiatives—a process described in the book *School Culture Rewired* (Gruenert & Whitaker, 2015).

The following might help explain the process using a smaller group of people. Imagine group A has eight people willing to change and two people unwilling to change. In group B, eight people are unwilling to change and two people are willing to change. Which group would change faster? Most of you would assume group A would change faster. However, since everyone has different levels of influence, imagine the two people (*outliers*) in both groups are opinion leaders; these are the teachers who the staff go to when there is a problem. Now which group has the capacity to change fastest? Group B now seems to have the influencers it needs in the right place. It gets messier when you think about relationships, history, and norms. Again, for the purposes of determining capacity to change and who the key players are, precision is not required.

Keep this in mind when hiring. Rather than thinking about hiring someone who will toe the line, maybe you should seek out and identify people who can offer fresh ideas for school improvement and be willing to sell them in social circles. Sometimes you need to add what you don't have versus just trying to increase the number of converts internally.

You should not try to change a culture until you know what kind of culture you have and the foundation it is built on. Plugging a destination into Google Maps without a starting point is as silly as making a change without a vision. Yet, some new school leaders who try to make changes quickly may face a strong culture unwilling to move. For example, if a school leader decides to create a more collaborative school culture, he or she must realize that there are many different ways to get this done, and there are many different versions of a collaborative culture. This leader must have a vision of what needs to be different. Imagine walking down your school hallways five years from now—what would you like to see? It's not so much a statement as it is something in your mind's eye, a destination that is real and you'll know when you get there. This type of change requires a great capacity to change, especially if it never existed in the past.

Sometimes a new leader makes a few changes in a weak culture only to find the changes had no direction, objective, or goal—just changes. If you want to find out what reaction an action might get, seek out changes in the climate and have a goal in mind. To mess with the culture just to test its strength will only make it stronger and more resistant to the next effort.

The Speed of Culture Change

Some societies seem to have an emphasized focus on speed—a trait everyone involved in professional sports teams to fast food restaurants values. The speed of culture change, however, is not something you can measure with a speedometer.

When you think of the *speed of culture change*, consider the following: (1) how fast a culture can indoctrinate members, (2) how fast a culture can grow into a force, and (3) how fast a culture can change without crashing.

The basis of this brief discussion is to challenge those who claim quite irrationally to change cultures faster than they are able to change. We see this often in sports when a new head coach tries to come in and change everything, hoping to make a big enough difference in the first year or two to keep his or her job. Rarely will we see a culture change within a year or two, because cultures simply cannot change that fast. *And you don't want them to change that fast.* And while you might see some things changing, those changes can feel like a culture change. It's important to note that there is no quick fix for an ineffective culture, period.

Cultures do not have the capacity to change quickly. Human belief systems can create dysfunction when there is too much change in a short period of time. The only relief will come from a regression to the way things were before the change. The pandemic reminds us of the value of "normal," and it had more than a year to impact the culture.

There are times and events that can hasten cultural change or at least provide a greater opportunity for it. Adding a new teacher to a school can impact culture. It's similar to someone getting married, and thus the family adds a son- or daughter-in-law to the mix. Family members may behave differently for a while, or they may alter their behavior forever. Maybe the new spouse communicates more effectively than the family members. It may be awkward at first, but this new person can also provide a role model for what the family wants communication among members to be like. Maybe the family didn't believe it was possible, but now members have a greater capacity to alter the family or home dynamic. Some families would appreciate the upgrade; some not so much. The new spouse first impacts his or her partner, and maybe the partner then impacts the family.

Similarly, a new teacher might first influence a grade level or department, and maybe it takes an altered veteran to influence his or her peers. If leaders don't take advantage of these opportunities, they run the risk of the culture flexing its muscles and allowing the organization or school to remain the same. In a school, the personalities and the roles of leaders—informal or not—can provide direction or limit influence. When these leaders are new, there is a true window for significant change to occur—first to the climate and then to the culture.

If you interview at a school that wants you to change the culture quickly, we recommend you don't take that job. If you promise to change the culture quickly as a way to get the job, you have overpromised, and you will most likely under-deliver. It probably is true, though, that you're in a better position to influence the culture as a new leader than the person who just left, especially if he or she had been there a while. You can share that you are definitely interested in improving the culture, but you'd like to start with the climate. Maybe that will help you seal the deal in the interview, assuming the administrators know the difference.

Conclusion

While you think about the next change, the magnitude of that change relative to your school's capacity to change is a valid consideration. It's also important to remember that change doesn't happen overnight. Any type of change takes time and patience; culture change especially can be a very challenging and slow process. When recruiting for school-improvement efforts, be sure to choose staff who do not have big egos, hidden obligations to uphold, or strong friendships with other members who may influence their objectivity. Try to take out your *gut feeling* about your staff's reaction to the next change and provide a more analytical approach to making that determination.

While the theory of capacity to change presented in this chapter may lack precision, it hopefully gives leaders a strategy to address the potential pushback from staff when things need to improve. By determining and examining a school's capacity to change, educators may be able to proceed at the most efficient and effective pace.

CHAPTER 7

School Culture Assessment

In some research studies, dissertations, and publications, we find authors arguing how best to change a culture. Some authors may claim that deliberately changing a culture is impossible and that you can only create conditions for culture change to happen. Some authors still confuse *culture* with *climate* and act as if leaders can change a culture within a few weeks. All this rhetoric places organizational culture as either a dependent variable or an independent variable. As a *dependent variable*, it becomes something you can change. As an *independent variable*, you can assume it remains constant—an unerring condition.

Many educators use instruments to measure or assess organizational cultures. What is missing in many of these scientific efforts is the qualitative aspect of any culture and how you might capture that information to make it useful. This chapter attempts to shed light on *qualitative research*—basically, the stories people tell—and how knowing something about this form of research increases your chances of understanding the type of culture you have relative to the one you need. It also examines how analyzing both quantitative and qualitative data can offer insight into the culture of any organization.

Qualitative Research

This section could have a multitude of citations from many researchers claiming the benefits or limitations of qualitative research. The *qualitative research approach* uses peoples' stories and experiences as data. There are many obvious limitations to this approach, mainly because people's stories are typically highly subjective, or others may contest them. Participants in qualitative research studies also may not live the same reality as others, so their versions of what happened may not be distinct.

Most qualitative researchers keep asking people the same questions until enough of them tell the same story (*saturation*) or until someone provides a unique perspective that reveals a new theme. In any case, qualitative researchers try to distill the high volume of information they collect into some key patterns and trends. Imagine a school leader approaching a faculty meeting by listening to and telling stories as the path to improvement.

Some might hear the word *subjective* and instantly develop an aversion to qualitative research—don't. You use qualitative methods every day when you ask people you like or trust for their opinions regarding a particular car, restaurant, person, movie, and so on. You listen to their opinions to gain insight into something you may be uncertain about. If researchers ask hundreds of people to complete a survey about a topic or concept, they call it *quantitative research*. In quantitative research, you try to establish an average, or mean, which tends to represent what is true for the majority.

Qualitative research asks people to share their stories. These people are often well informed about the topic. After listening to enough stories about the same topic, you can begin to draw out some common patterns and trends. You can ask 1,000 people to rate a restaurant in town using a survey, or you can ask a few friends in a casual manner and potentially dig deeper with follow-up questions. You must decide which method suits your school environment best.

Qualitative research is an art. It takes a long time to develop trust among participants. Even then, participants might not be completely able to articulate what actually happened. The researcher must be able to listen without reacting and probe deeper without causing discomfort. Imagine trying to get ineffective teachers in a school to disclose their inability to help students learn. You couldn't ask, "Are you a good teacher?" and expect a self-searching, honest response.

When conducting qualitative research, we like to use *observations* and *interviews* together. Whether we see something or ask about something, it is good practice to inquire further by looking for anything that might support what we saw or heard. Strong leaders already do this to some degree.

Themes

After spending time in a new school, one can eventually sense patterns and trends that seem to separate a group from other groups. With qualitative research, we call patterns and trends *themes*. For example, in a restaurant setting, a manager might have employees that value friendliness, safety, and healthy foods. Another restaurant manager in the same franchise just five miles away might not value cleanliness or friendliness. In one school, the themes may relate to kindness, caring, passion for students, and parent input. In another school, which may be five miles down the road, themes may relate to territories, competition, testing, and watching the clock. Themes help you better understand what is happening in an organization. You can discover what is most important to the people there. You can learn how they solve problems. And you can learn more about their culture than the members may be aware of.

Observations

The interactions among adults in a school may be the most telling evidence of the type of culture that exists relative to what a typology might identify (see the typology activity in Gruenert & Whitaker, 2015). Interactions among students are not as critical, and the interactions between students and adults are less critical than listening to how teachers talk to one another. The stories people tell in school illustrates a lot about those schools, much like an anthropologist studying any kind of group around the world.

Other adults in the building contribute to the school culture. The support staff who have been there a long time may be some of the best people to watch or listen to when certain topics emerge, but the veteran teachers who have been there the longest are the ones who ultimately determine how things are done. Consequently, school researchers will spend most of their time observing teachers in and out of classrooms to get the best picture of the culture. The following are the places and times that seem to provide the most and best information.

- **Classrooms:** Classrooms may be the most visited venue when the research topic is school improvement or teacher evaluation—whether it is a principal doing a scheduled or unscheduled observation, teachers learning from other teachers, or for research purposes. Here, you can observe teacher-student interactions too. From these observations, you can build many patterns and trends that not only reveal how a teacher instructs but also, to some degree, the type of school or classroom culture that may be in place.

- **Hallways:** Hallways are places where teachers interact with other teachers, usually in view of students, administrators, parents, and support staff, which might impose a degree of politeness you won't find in more informal situations. The way teachers choose to interact among themselves and with students in the school or any public area demonstrates something about the school's culture.

- **Lunch:** Lunch is an informal time that can expose unwritten teacher territories. Where a teacher chooses to eat lunch and with whom says something about the school's culture as well as potential subcultures. Additionally, any time there is a group, there are *power chairs* and *emotionally reserved seating*—even if these teachers arrive late, no one will dare sit in their seats. Schools can be very similar to churches or other places where people sit in the same seats on a regular basis. Though this could be thought of as a habit, people react in different ways if someone sits in their self-assigned spots.

- **Formal meetings:** Formal meetings, such as faculty meetings, are places where collaboration and competition can collide. We typically try to help school staff become more collaborative, a positive culture trait, which works best when formal structures do not force teachers to work together. Forcing collaboration is a more contrived type of culture that usually crashes when people have had enough.

- **Informal gatherings:** These are the places where most teachers can be themselves. Here, they express their opinions without worrying about backlash. These are places where they can vent and share what they think is working and what isn't. If we hear teachers talking about how to be better teachers in an informal setting (that is, *talking about student achievement when they do not have to*), this is an effective school.

Interviews

Asking people about their experiences during interviews can be a limited way of determining what is actually happening at a school, and yet it is through stories that cultures live. When researching culture, the trick is to discover the culture without actually asking about the culture. You could ask direct questions. For example, a school researcher could stand up in a faculty meeting and bluntly ask teachers if they have an effective culture. *Yes* or *no*? Done. No one is under the illusion that this would be an effective strategy.

Design interview questions that allow participants to express their values and beliefs—not just their feelings. Responses to these questions should get to the deepest level of culture—what Schein (1985) calls *assumptions*. The best interview questions will tap into the "way we do things around here." Much like a psychiatrist, ask interviewees what happened, why they think it happened, and what they were thinking. Invite them to share any stories that can support these behaviors.

Data Analysis

In this chapter, we introduced the qualitative research method to help you better understand school culture, perhaps challenging school leaders to think about schools in a more folklore way, and maybe less of a quantitative way. The challenge is to combine the *quantitative* data (numbers in tables and spreadsheets) with the *qualitative* data (stories, observations, and interviews), hoping to reveal the latent values and beliefs that drive a particular group. *The values and beliefs are the foundation of any culture.* What makes this combined approach to school improvement interesting is that group members may be unaware of the themes driving their work. They may claim "it is simply how we do things around here," and nobody ever questions what they do. In other words, holding up the mirror to reveal unknown themes can cause some schools to self-reflect and thus, self-correct.

One obvious challenge about trying to examine a school culture from a qualitative perspective is the neutrality of the observer. No one can ever be completely neutral, but it is especially challenging if the observer is someone internal (within the school). Having someone from outside the school (and potentially the district) may be the best way to gather specific data and stories.

We often find school leaders insisting that the school must improve without any sense of where faculty and staff are or knowing when they have arrived at their destination. While it may sound easy, describing the type of culture you need can be a challenge. You can read stories of other school leaders who have changed their schools. You can read about theories stating how to optimize your current culture. The real challenge is taking this information and making it work in your school, with your teachers.

Conclusion

Assessing school culture can be quite a challenge. That's why many things that claim to measure culture at best help determine or describe school climate. While this has value, it is clearly not measure of culture. Being able to accurately assess a culture requires a deft touch and a high level of understanding about what comprises a culture. Usually, it takes an outsider to have a neutral eye to actually see the components of a school culture. Understanding the culture of a school is an essential step to help move a culture, and the school, in a positive direction.

CHAPTER 8

The Necessity of Culture Change

In some schools, teachers are ready and willing to share ideas and resources. In this type of culture, people view their world as an unlimited sum game. They feel that sharing has an exponential benefit and the more one person grows, the more everyone grows. However, some schools and teachers view the world as a limited sum game. That is, when they share an idea, it is one less for them.

In some education settings, it is safe to be vulnerable, express limitations, and ask others for assistance. In others, the people who do these things are seen as weak or ineffective. They might even be ridiculed. Positive culture change is an essential element of school improvement.

If a school's culture needs to change, it's reasonable to assume that it's because it promotes inefficacy at a destructive level. Anything less than destructive inefficacy may not require a culture change. Some problems may not need a culture change to fix. You should not consider changing the culture an experiment, an innovation, or a response to a few negative teachers. Changing the culture is the equivalent of performing major brain surgery—a doctor should only perform a major surgery after he or she exhausts all other options.

For example, cutting down the number of cigarettes one smokes a day is a world away from cutting out smoking entirely. Or if one wants to be more conscious of the foods he she eats, that is less of an intrusion on his or her life than to go completely vegan. If a school leader wants to get the faculty to care more about their students' mental health, that does not require a culture change as long as the faculty already care about the students. However, that leader might need a culture change if teachers do not care at all. Changing something teachers already do, increasing or decreasing a task or activity, is different from introducing a new element into the system.

Consider whether or not the culture *supports* the problems. You can fix many problems without having to reframe the whole system, yet it seems vogue for leaders to announce they will change the culture.

This chapter discusses how to identify the need for culture change. Even when the need is obvious, some cultures may be so embedded, they're nearly impossible to change. This doesn't mean, however, that school improvement is not possible through changing elements of the climate. Sometimes you will receive warning signs that alert you to the need for culture change, but other times the signs are not as obvious. Paying close attention to these warning signs will help you understand when the culture is telling you there is a problem that needs to be fixed.

Unchangeable Cultures

It's important to accept that you may not get a chance to change the culture. Few principals get contracts for three to five years, even though research says it takes at least five years "to engage a school's community, change its culture, and improve its teaching" (Hill, Mellon, Laker, & Goddard, 2017). Moreover, the research on principal length of tenure is clear and consistent: the average principal works at a school for less than three years (National Association of Secondary School Principals, 2021). The mathematics don't add up when a school leader wants to change a culture, given he or she may be gone in less than three years. This begs the question: If you were given less than three years to change or improve the culture of a school, what would you do?

Again, a new leader may not need to change the culture to improve the school. What can a new principal do with less than three years as the leader? Certainly most new principals are familiar with the process of strategic planning, which usually spans well into five or more years. A common phrase allegedly attributed to management consultant and educator Peter Drucker states: "Culture eats strategy for breakfast" (as cited in Forbes, 2015). In other words, no matter whatever course you set for your school or organization, the culture (how people behave and what they believe) determines what happens. New principals should identify problems they can address to improve a school that do not require culture shifts. Maybe shifting the climate is sufficient or is, at the very least, a good place to start.

The culture manages relationships in most schools. It's possible to make friends with anyone in the school building, but befriending someone who does not conform within cultural constraints might cause you to be labeled as an outlier. Just like the culture, these clubs are somewhat invisible—the more invisible, the more influence they have.

If you know the major players or influencers in a culture, it may be possible to make things happen *in that culture*. Remember, it is possible to improve a school without changing the culture. The following actions try to shed light on what might constitute climate changes that will not shake the culture in a major way but potentially improve the school nonetheless.

- Shift members in teams; put a parent on a team.
- Make the décor friendlier in the teacher workroom.
- Keep the equipment teachers use in good condition.
- Shift teachers' classrooms, duties, or committee assignments.
- Co-facilitate individualized education programs (IEPs).
- Let teachers run and own the faculty meetings.
- Build a trophy case for teacher accomplishments.
- Encourage students and alumni to let teachers know when they make a difference.

These may be changes in one or two elements of the culture or the climate. They are not wholesale culture changes, but they could be if they become how we do things around here. To change a culture is to dig deep into the reasons teachers believe they are there. The culture represents what is most important; this does not change with charisma, money, or teacher evaluations.

There are leaders who claim the ability to change a culture quickly. Their efforts may change the school, and things can improve without them changing the culture. Chances are that anything they think can happen quickly will be more appealing, but it isn't a culture change, which means it is vulnerable to reverting back just as rapidly. Use the climate as a barometer when you decide to make changes. Use changes in the climate as small tests to reveal the strength of the culture. The culture will quickly tell you what matters most, pay attention to the pushback. Listen and observe the major players or influencers. These are the rules of the game.

Chances are if you are in a successful school, you can make a few changes in the climate pretty easily. Listen for the funny stories people tell, as some cultures will allow stories of others' failures to seem funny and a lesson learned. A negative culture can start as a few teachers sarcastically sharing stories of a few teachers or students who are struggling, which gives permission for others to share their stories of others struggling. You know you have a *negative culture* if staff share these stories regularly.

You know you have a *toxic culture* if the leaders share these stories, or worse, start them. Pay attention to what staff considers funny in your school. Do staff laugh with people or at them? When they hear of another teacher's successes, do staff celebrate with him or her or feel jealousy and also need to point out the teacher's faults? Think of the culture you want in your own school and classrooms. Isn't that exactly what you desire in your school?

Warning Signs

Since 1996, most vehicles come with a computer that can warn drivers when there is a problem. The warning is usually an attention-getting light on your dashboard. The manual suggests you go to the nearest repair shop and have mechanics check out the light. Sometimes you drive for many days with a warning light on, almost to the point of not paying much attention to it anymore. You know there is an issue, but you become very good at ignoring it.

The warning light might indicate something needs fixing in the near future, or it could be something that needs attention very quickly. If you continue to drive with the warning light on, you are taking a chance. Similarly, school leaders may be taking chances when they ignore organizational climate warning signs. Some signs may be more critical than others.

Some car problems are obvious, like a flat tire or brakes wearing out. A noise or vibration will make driving difficult. We like to think of the school's climate as those noises that indicate a problem you must address right away. On the other hand, only those who understand the concept of school culture and know their culture can diagnose hidden problems (that do not make noise).

A good culture survey may not pick up on climate issues. The group may have acclimated to a negative climate. It is difficult to identify ineffective behaviors, values, or beliefs if the culture tells you they are effective. If, as the leader of a school, you have had problems with the culture and have been there a long time, you are probably not going to see what needs to change—you have been ignoring the warning lights on the dashboard too long and you are now trusting that the problems are not problems or they do not exist. If the principal becomes blind to warning lights and eventually deaf to the warning noises, so will the whole school staff.

Beware of those who promise results or guarantee success when it comes to changing the culture of a school. There are many ways to improve a school; deciding what is most important will determine how difficult the change may be. Unfortunately, some schools are unable to determine what is most important, which can make most anything most important. That oft-repeated phrase is also one of the truest: if you can't count what is important, you make what you can count important (Ageling, 2018). Don't feel like every problem needs a new culture.

Conclusion

Although school cultures inherently do not want to change, it is critical for schools to continue to move forward in a positive direction. The path may not be linear, but it must result in growth. Some cultures are much more challenging than others, but all of them take time to move. When leadership has consistent turnover, there can be a tendency to wait the new one out. This, in and of itself, enables the culture to resist improvement.

Just like the goal of a school is to help every student achieve his or her potential, the goal of leaders and educators must be to help the school and its culture achieve its potential. Acknowledging the difficulty of the path ahead may result in more patience for the process and give value to small steps toward success.

CHAPTER 9

A Closer Look at Values

Values and culture are inherently linked. If we value something, then the culture recognizes and celebrates that value. Our values are what are most important to us, and we typically belong to a culture because others in that culture share those values. In *School Culture Rewired* (Gruenert & Whitaker, 2015), we identify twelve elements of culture:

- Climate
- Mission and vision
- Language
- Humor

- Routines, rituals, and ceremonies
- Norms
- Rules
- Symbols

- Stories
- Heroes
- Values
- Beliefs (p. 28)

In this chapter, we focus on perhaps one of the most important elements in any culture—values. *Values* are what a group of people hold most dear and can draw a group of people together, keep them together as a bonding mechanism, as well as create separation from other groups.

School culture usually only becomes an important topic of discussion when someone is looking to change it. For some, changing the lunch schedule or the lunch menu can feel like culture change, while for others, changing the curriculum or adopting a new student grading software feels like culture change. Actually, neither are culture changes, but they can definitely impact the climate. You can try to change the whole culture, make a substantial change, or just make a dent. Regardless of the level of culture change you seek, the values of the school serve as a framework for change or resistance to change.

Our values are a reflection of what we hold to be most important in life. Being aware of those values can help us identify what kind of culture we desire as well. This applies both in our personal and professional lives. Sometimes we need to actually sit down and think about what we value most at home and at work to realize what kind of culture is best.

What's Most Important in Life

In this section, we hope to reveal what is most important to you in your personal and professional lives. While many of us share the same top-ten values, a shift in values is a shift in culture. When a school decides to change its culture, it really means a shift in values. Before continuing, we suggest you complete the quick questionnaire in figure 9.1.

This activity might become more difficult as you move further away from the first non-negotiable. Before examining your work culture, consider the strength of culture for a moment. To change a whole culture, which is always difficult, it would feel like changing any item in your top-three list. While some may allow numbers one and two to vacillate on occasion, whenever someone tries to force you to replace any of the first three non-negotiables, it hurts—you will push back with whatever you can to resist.

A proposed change in your top three might be to allow something new to take the place of your number-one item. This does not mean making a number four or six a number one or two; it means replacing number one with something not in your top ten—making something you rarely think about more important than anything else in your life, which means something already in your top three must go. The same feelings of resistance will arise in staff, even when you try to add something proven beneficial.

Some cultures have built up so much staff resilience to change that any proposed change will suffer great failure. To make a change within the culture suggests a reprioritization of existing values. This is less damaging than trying to completely extinguish a value, which means you will get less pushback from staff. This is moving a number four, five, or six into the top three. You will get pushback from those who feel like number one or two is being completely thrown out. Again, this is about reprioritizing values and the challenges leaders face when trying to change a culture; leaders are usually trying to shift or change a value or values.

If it is a *weak culture*, meaning staff are not on the same page, the changes will be less dramatic, and the institutionalized values have less meaning to what staff do. There will be little agreement as to what the top three values are at the school, which makes the culture weak—a necessary ingredient to successful change. A strong culture will

List the three most important things in your life right now. These are your *non-negotiables*—or the things you can become very defensive about when anyone messes with them.

    1.

    2.

    3.

List the next three most important things in your life.

    4.

    5.

    6.

List the next four most important things in your life.

    7.

    8.

    9.

    10.

Figure 9.1: The most important things in your life.

*Visit **go.SolutionTree.com/schoolimprovement** for a free reproducible version of this figure.*

not allow change as much as a weak culture will. Thus, leaders need to weaken (not make ineffective, just weaken) their cultures for a change to have any chance of surviving. In a weak culture, changes will matter to some people but not to most. And if those the change most affects are the least influential, they may offer little resistance.

When leaders speak of a culture change, they usually mean making a few shifts in the culture, perhaps changing a few routines or habits. These small changes require some support from opinion leaders, but as long as the changes do not impact the top three or four values, any pushback may be short lived. A small change goes a long way later when the leader must change one of the top three elements the staff most value in their culture. Sometimes even climate changes—having a cleaner school, painting faded walls, adding new signage, and so on, can help set the table for more significant change acceptance. With a history of successful ideas, the bank account now has capital to invest in more new ideas.

What's Most Important at Work

Let's return to the original list of ten most important things in your life from figure 9.1 (page 115). Did your work at school make the list? If some form of being an effective educator or leader did not make your top ten, then this chapter may not make much sense. It may also demonstrate that a few things at work might be burning you out.

Now, repeat the activity in figure 9.1 using figure 9.2. This time, focus on your work as an educator. List the top three things in your work that are most important to you, and then list the next three, and then list the final four.

You would expect the two lists of what's most important to have some alignment. Cultures gain strength when the people believe in what they are doing. Too much misalignment could be a recipe for frustration and possible burnout. Over the long haul, a misalignment of what is important (when what we value at home does not match what is valued at work) can lead to the school's culture becoming toxic.

Value Change to Culture Change

Now we'll address the power of school culture and values when people try to change them. If it sounds like school leaders want to change the culture, they just might be looking to impress people with jargon. No schools have entirely negative cultures—where everything the staff do, value, and believe is 100 percent negative or a source of trouble. Instead, there are usually a few detrimental behaviors preventing what the staff is hoping to accomplish, such as establishing routines or habits, or

List the three most important things in your work as an educator right now. These are your *non-negotiables*—or the things you can become very defensive about when anyone messes with them.

1.

2.

3.

List the next three most important things in your work.

4.

5.

6.

List the next four most important things in your work.

7.

8.

9.

10. .

Figure 9.2: The most important things in your work.

*Visit **go.SolutionTree.com/schoolimprovement** for a free reproducible version of this figure.*

improving the climate. You can address these issues with shifts or dents to the culture, meaning you can move a few things from less important to more important without touching the top three or four things you value most. You can change a few values without changing the culture, but you cannot change the culture without changing your values. For example, consider the following sample educator top-ten list.

1. Student safety
2. Student learning
3. Student health
4. Teacher safety
5. Teacher health
6. Teacher effectiveness
7. Positive school climate
8. Strong support staff
9. Supportive parents
10. Working technology

Imagine trying to impose number eight, nine, or ten in to the top three. It would be easier to put four, five, or six in the top three than eight, nine, or ten. If your staff were to value parent support over student safety, you can imagine what the pushback might feel like in any school. Yet is it possible some staffs might try this? Is it possible some staffs might try to do this with whatever the flavor of the month is or move something into the top three because a few loud voices demand it?

Making plans to change values that are far down on the list, perhaps number twenty-five or thirty, does not change or even shift the culture. These might include improving the appearance of the building, getting new trash cans in all the classes, or adding items to the lunch menu.

It is disheartening when we hear people who profess to be experts in school culture offering to sell a "new culture of [insert whatever the latest trend is]," as if someone could order culture change like something off a menu. What's even worse is that some staff may believe there are blank spaces to fill in the organization's top ten. We hope to shed light on what leaders mean despite what they may say relative to school culture change. To know the difference is to act different.

Remember, you cannot change a culture by creating a new one. There is already a culture there, and it took a long time for it to evolve. It will not go away without a fight. Whatever you want the new culture to be, it will actually be a hybrid of what you already have. You never get to go back to zero and start over. Be optimistic about the change you need, and be realistic about the effort it will take.

It does little good to learn new methods to help English learners be successful, to help teachers write a better IEP, or better align the curriculum to assessment standards if the staff does not value these things. It is rare for one teacher to embrace something new, stand alone, and be successful. Leaders need a tremendous amount of support for when the naysayers fight back. That is why knowing about the concept of school culture, how it can change, and then how to strengthen it are necessary prior to investing in innovative professional development.

Know your values. Know your non-negotiables.

Conclusion

In order to understand a school's culture, it's essential to know what the school and its people value. These values are directly linked to the resulting culture. To change or improve a culture, it might be best to alter the values first. Values, just like the culture, can dig in strongest when they are threatened. Leaders and everyone involved in helping a culture move forward must be sensitive to this link between values and culture.

CHAPTER 10

Not the Perfect Culture, the *Right* Culture

Effective leaders are not looking for the *perfect* culture (there is no such thing); they are looking for the *right* culture—the right culture for their schools, teachers, students, and communities. Often, leaders find marketers or organizations trying to sell them a culture—for example, a culture proven to raise test scores and lower discipline issues, or maybe one that guarantees teacher effectiveness, innovation, and collaboration. Any school can become strong in these elements, but it will not look the same from school to school.

The most effective schools will have a faculty that work as a team, but unfortunately, many cultures believe a strong team needs a "star" to function (Schein, 2009). Many professional sports teams glorify this belief. A star on the basketball team can average thirty points, but the team can still lose every game. The coach can ensure he or she plays this star all the time and limits the minutes of the less skilled teammates, thus the team becomes overly dependent on one person to carry the whole load. The school leader could assign all the star students to the school's star teacher. We cannot imagine any school leader would think this was a good idea. To build the right culture, leaders need the *right* people, not just the stars.

In the right culture, school leaders recognize what is needed, understand who is best suited to perform which tasks, and know who should not be asked to do certain tasks. Every school employs different people and personalities, each having a variety of talents, work ethics, and limitations. The ingredients to a great school may be similar, but the actual recipes are very different. This is why different organizations need different approaches and different cultures.

In this chapter, we examine what the right school culture looks like, a culture in which good things happen for both teachers and students. This is what schools should strive for. By learning to understand culture and climate, it's easier to know how to create the culture that is appropriate for your school.

What the Right School Culture Looks Like

In the most effective school cultures, the right ones, staff attitudes and mindsets match the direction staff want to go—good chemistry between personnel, mission, and vision. There is success, but not without some stress. There is collaboration and autonomy. There is trust, hope, forgiveness, and commitment.

There are many ways to think about school culture and climate. The use of analogies (from previous chapters) may help you understand the differences and similarities between the two concepts as you reach for the right culture for your school and staff. With the right culture, there is a connection between what staff truly commit to and what they actually devote a lot of time and energy to. Ask yourself how much time, energy, resources, and thinking you devote to your job.

Some people overinvest in their jobs to a fault, perhaps lacking a life outside work. The regime of world-class athletes might give you an idea of what extreme commitment looks like. But there is a cost to always trying to be the best. We also know people who simply go to work to collect a paycheck. Their personal investment in their careers is practically nil. Both types of people are rare, but they provide a sense of balance when talking about culture change. The following three examples should shed some light on what it means to have the *right* culture.

EXAMPLE ONE
Know the Players

If we look at a particularly negative school culture (one driven by large egos, marked territories, and self-indulgences by a few toxic teachers), we can predict what its informal leaders will do or say given just about any situation. It's like playing chess against someone who is predictable. These players never blindside you; and you don't actually respect what they do, you leverage it.

If you know Mr. Smith hates any type of professional development activity, you should probably not let him get too close to those who value it or those who you would like to value it. If Ms. Juarez does not develop particularly good relationships with parents, you probably should not let her help make decisions about your next parent activity. You may have teachers who do not design lessons well, some who always send students to the office, and some who do not want new teachers to be successful. Knowing who these people are can make school improvement easier to negotiate than not knowing.

The same way the most effective teachers have an intentionality to their actions, so do the most effective leaders. A quality teacher would not let three disruptive students sit together at the back of the class. A quality leader increases or decreases faculty interactions when possible—assigning mentors, plan times, room locations, and so on to facilitate close proximity of new teachers to the most effective teachers. In the following example, having the right culture starts with knowing what kind of culture you have and who the players are, and using many of the existing, internal unwritten rules to your benefit.

EXAMPLE TWO
Stuck in Tradition

In sports, sometimes a new coach with a successful past at another organization struggles with a new team that also has a successful past. For any number of reasons, the chemistry between the coach and the team does not click or gel soon enough, and the team owner gets nervous and fires the coach. In this example, we share the struggles of a successful principal who is new to a successful school. The match may seem perfect at first, but never forget the impact of chemistry on outcomes.

Dr. Williams came to the school as the third principal in more than fifty years. She was familiar with the pride the teachers had regarding past successes and was eager to get started. She brought a virtual toolkit from her previous school, where the staff also had many successes. After a few weeks into the school year, it became clear to the principal that no one was to touch or even discuss changing school traditions. The culture was strong, and teachers were not willing to risk changing any piece of it. With each nudge at changing the culture, Dr. Williams felt herself losing credibility with the staff.

This school was not the right culture for Dr. Williams, and she did not want to invest much emotion or effort into making it like her previous school. She realized that whoever came in as principal should simply leave everything alone, and the school would run itself, with a level of success for many years to come. Dr. Williams is a more active leader who wants to work in a place that values her input and is willing to experiment. Again, not a good fit. She could have fought the staff over the next few years and maybe won over a few teachers, but she wanted something else. This was not a failure of Dr. Williams as the new principal, or the staff; the school simply did not have the right culture for her.

EXAMPLE THREE

Ready for Change

A school's young faculty is hoping to implement some exciting ideas they have been generating. Given the many retirements and teachers promoted to administrative positions, the school's culture is weak, meaning that it is vulnerable to change (but not necessarily ineffective). One of those staff promoted is Mr. Gomez, who became the new building principal. He had been a teacher at this school for five years and served as assistant principal the previous year. There are still a few veteran teachers who are not thrilled about possible changes, but Mr. Gomez met with them the previous year to discuss how they might be valuable to these changes.

This school's culture is the right culture for what the faculty want to do with their new ideas. The changes coming will not change the culture, as it is already the culture they need. Had the new principal been unfamiliar with the school vision and hadn't built trust with the veteran faculty, his or her proposed changes may have been difficult to achieve. Making big changes in a school does not always mean changing the culture. Some changes need the right culture; some cultures need the right changes.

Additional Thoughts for Identifying the Right School Culture

Leaders can improve schools with the culture they have while at the same time improving the culture. The culture you have already has a social structure made up of several smaller networks. Faculty and staff obey unwritten rules, most based on stories or myths from the past. Knowing and understanding these unwritten rules is like knowing your opponent's next five moves in chess, allowing you to play to that set of rules, which can make your strategies more successful.

Following are some additional thoughts to help you understand the particular culture at your school.

- **If there is a right culture, there is a wrong culture:** The wrong culture is not always the one with obvious dysfunctions or an abundance of toxic staff. The wrong culture could be the one you try to copy from another school because the staff there seem to have a lot of success.

- **Culture always wins:** Leaders need to learn how to use the culture they have rather than always wanting to change it. An education buzzword is *innovation*. If you need to innovate, innovate, innovate, when do you stop? If your school is successful, do you get rid of your culture and innovate some more? Some cultures claim that failure is not an option. Another culture might claim that if you are not failing, you are not trying hard enough. Some educators are a better fit for one of these schools than others.

Conclusion

Different organizations have, and need, different cultures. Being aware of this is a first step to identifying and moving toward a culture that is best for your school as well as your classroom; in other words, the *right* culture. With the right culture, staff connect and commit to cultural norms because they match up with their personal values and beliefs. By being aware of how climate and culture are connected, educators can be more effective in choosing and moving toward what is best for their classrooms and schools, finding the right cultural fit.

Epilogue

You may be thinking about what to do next to make improvements in your school culture. Consider the following as a sort of playbook. But first, we want to reinforce some important concepts to keep in mind as you lead people to improve school culture.

Before You Begin

Before you begin any kind of school improvement efforts, it's essential to examine the culture and climate of the school, and know the difference between the two. You might be aiming to improve the climate of the school, but you also might want to make larger cultural changes that have a larger impact. Consider the following before you get started.

- If the principal is new to a school (less than three years), many staff will still remember how things were done in the past with the previous principal. Staff will compare much of what a new principal does to what the previous principal did. It may not matter how effective the past principal was as much as how that principal made staff feel. You can have happy, not to mention satisfied, teachers in an ineffective school.

- The most difficult part of change is convincing staff they need to change. Having teachers who want to change reduces about 90 percent of the challenges and problems from these efforts. Note that *wanting* to change the culture is different from actually *changing* the culture.

- The assumptions staff bring to work influence how they behave at work. Educators should be aware of what staff believe about learning and teaching, and consider how those beliefs influence their decisions and practices.

- There may be problems at your school that have been there for so long they become difficult to recognize as problems. The school climate is rarely the root cause and conducting a climate audit may not be the way to reveal any real problems.

- Anyone can change the attitude of a group for a short period of time. But it takes a sustained effort and commitment from school leaders for a temporary change to become the catalyst for a change in a school culture. Doing something new or for the first time does not change a culture. If you do something once, it impacts the climate. If you never stop doing it, it may impact the culture.

- Sometimes teachers close their doors (emotionally or physically) before class begins. There may be several reasons for this, and few of those reasons will point to an effective school. If teachers want a different classroom culture this year, it is up to them. If effective teachers shut their doors, it is a sign that the building culture is not any help. This is the opposite of a collaborative culture.

- School leaders may become impatient because real culture change moves along at a snail's pace. Yet, any organization set up to accommodate a quick change will also be vulnerable to a negative change. Too much capacity to change can result in a group chasing every shiny penny it sees.

- Getting no pushback is not a good sign. Levels of job satisfaction do not change a culture. A change in satisfaction can simply be an indicator that something is happening or nothing is happening. For every problem, there is a *happy person* hoping the problem stays, maybe because it supports their agenda or their unwillingness to change.

- If a school leader dreads presenting anything in this book to the faculty, there is a problem. Professional development should be fun, and new teachers should learn to look forward to those events. Each school will have a few teachers who are against any change, so leaders should not design school-improvement strategies or plans around these people.

- To study organizational culture is interesting if you are curious why people do the things they do in groups. However, understanding how a culture impacts a group is not very helpful in improving schools if the staff does not have the capacity to change. If school leaders attempt to make changes to the culture without knowing all that may be involved to prepare staff for change, they can make a negative culture stronger.

- The power of culture is that it hides and whispers in people's ears regarding what is most important and valued in a school. Culture and climate are in people's minds. The challenge then becomes changing peoples' minds and attitudes.

- Leaders should not change the culture until they know what they *have* relative to what they *need*. Do not think of culture change as an experiment, innovation, or response to a few negative teachers. It is like major brain surgery. Do not confuse it with improving what staff already do.

- Beware of school leaders who promise positive results or guarantee success when it comes to changing the school culture. You cannot change a culture by creating a new one. There is already a culture there, and it took a long time for it to become *the* culture.

- As noted earlier, you can change a few values without changing the culture, but you cannot change the culture without changing your values. The culture's job is to get everyone on the same page, respecting the same values. The best way to shift a value is through a story.

- With the right culture, there is a connection between what leaders truly commit to and what they spend a lot of time and energy doing. Give teachers what they signed up for.

- Making big improvements in a school does not always mean changing the culture. Changing the culture does not guarantee improvement.

The following questions might help you to imagine the first steps in the process of changing the culture at your school. In the book *School Culture Rewired*, we present additional ideas, especially if you want to establish a baseline for culture change (Gruenert & Whitaker, 2015).

- Identify and recruit your most effective teachers in your efforts. Let them help you create the vision of the culture you want.

- List the reasons your more effective teachers choose to stay (chapter 9, page 113), and use those reasons to bond the group. Use these values and beliefs to try to encourage ineffective teachers who might be discouraged or feel alienated to make improvements and join the others. Let the effective teachers be the ones who tell the stories. In leadership, a good story is better than great information.

- Determine what type of classroom culture you have and the behaviors you want to change (chapter 4, page 51).

- Determine your staff's capacity to change (chapter 6, page 87). Cultures evolve relative to the supply and demand of leaders.

- Pay attention to the climate (chapter 3, page 43). How staff feel is very important. Leaders must let staff know when they are wrong and show them a better way to accomplish their goal without losing their passion for teaching or trust of others. They should guide and encourage ineffective or negative staff or educators to improve and provide a means for them to collaborate.

- Recognize the indicators of culture change as well as the climate elements that you may mistake for culture (chapter 3, page 43, and chapter 8, page 107). Culture change is not simply rearranging what is already there.

- If you do not feel ready to approach culture change or improvements, don't try it. Do not count on random behaviors. It won't be perfect; perfection is the enemy of excellence (Cairns, n.d.). There are different types of collaborative school cultures. Some may be more progressive than others, but this does not reflect overall effectiveness. Collaboration makes it faster for the organization to learn from its mistakes.

- Be patient. If things are moving fast and easy, it is not the culture that is changing. It may be the climate, and this may be an essential preliminary step to real school improvement.

The Playbook for Culture Change

What is your next move? Well, first address the issue of what is in *your* mind. To change the culture of an organization requires a committed and sustained effort, as there will be many staff, as well as nuances in the school, which will challenge the effort. The principal needs to be more resilient than the culture.

While a playbook will have options, it rarely lists these options in any order. The environment (the other team, negative teachers) determines the plays, which reveals what it is trying to protect or prevent. As a principal or any school leader who is considering a culture change, you should know who and how these negative teachers will fight the change. You should recruit the most effective teachers to support each move you make, without creating the perception that those teachers are part of an elite, private principal's club. Know the rules of the game, and do not try to change any of these rules too fast. Know what is important to the current staff, and try not to remove the sacred parts of the culture too fast.

For many principals, it will be easy to claim there are too many other things to do and changing a culture takes too much time. This is the culture rewarding the principal for being too busy to change the culture. You should not become frustrated when the culture does not change, as members of the culture design it to resist change.

Part of the playbook is acknowledging that you cannot change or determine when it is time to try something else.

As part of your playbook, consider using the activities listed in figure E.1.

Activity	How This Leads to Culture Change or Improvement
What Is Your School Culture Doing? (figure 1.1, page 19)	This activity helps you understand what your culture is doing relative to the notion of effectiveness.
Classroom Culture Assessment (figure 4.2, page 68)	You cannot ignore the concept of culture at the classroom level. This assessment is the first step in both understanding and possibly improving your classroom culture.
Introductions Scorecard (figure 5.1, page 79)	This activity allows you to quantify the things you see in other people, which you value or not, when you interact with others.
Comparing and Contrasting Classroom Scorecards (figure 5.3, page 84)	This activity allows the best classroom cultures to serve as resources for all other classrooms.
Assessment for Individual Capacity to Change (figure 6.1, page 91)	Leaders need to be able to identify people who have the capacity to change in order to evaluate whether the school itself has that same capacity. This activity will help you assess that capacity.
Assessment for Individual Social Influence (figure 6.2, page 92)	Leaders need to know who teachers trust when change approaches a school. This activity can help you identify those people.
Organizational Capacity to Change Graphic Example (figure 6.6, page 96)	Not having the capacity to change will sabotage the next attempt to improve. There are key people involved in this process, which this figure points out.
The Most Important Things in Your Life (figure 9.1, page 115)	This activity asks you to identify the non-negotiables and determine if there are conflicts in how work can influence your quality of life.
The Most Important Things in Your Work (figure 9.2, page 117)	This activity asks you to find out if the things you value at work align with your personal values.

Figure E.1: Activities for school improvement.

*Visit **go.SolutionTree.com/schoolimprovement** for a free reproducible version of this figure.*

These activities focus on *starting and sustaining conversations* (a qualitative approach to school improvement) that reveal your culture. Hopefully the value of stories, and who is telling those stories become just as important as any spreadsheet with student data when thinking about improving a school. Each activity should generate stories, routines, norms, and beliefs (and some numbers) that reveal the culture and give you some idea of what your ideal culture might look like.

Educators perpetuate the status quo when they choose not to talk about their culture. Some of these activities may give you a peek into what an optimal culture may look like in your school, but it will probably look different in every school. Returning to some of these activities a year later may help to see if you are moving in the right direction. This process is most successful if your most effective teachers are the ones facilitating activities like these and what a collaborative school culture demands.

Conclusion

Becoming aware of and developing an understanding of the meaning of school culture and school climate are essential first steps in school-improvement strategies. Being aware of where they connect and where they do not is essential to understand how to approach school improvement. You can make a real difference when you can improve both climate and culture, creating classrooms and schools that foster learning in all students. It is a challenging path, but one well worth taking. Thank you for choosing to make a difference in every school and each classroom. Your impact is significant.

References and Resources

Ageling, W.-J. (2018, July 6). If you can't count what's important you make what you can count important . . . *Medium*. Accessed at https://medium.com/agile-insights/if-you-cant-count -what-s-important-you-make-what-you-can-count-important-62f8171abc1e on May 14, 2021.

Banas, J. A., Dunbar, N., Rodriguez, D., & Liu, S.-J. (2011). A review of humor in educational settings: Four decades of research. *Communication Education*, *60*(1), 115–144.

Barker, E. (2017). *Barking up the wrong tree: The surprising science behind why everything you know about success is (mostly) wrong.* New York: HarperOne.

Barth, R. S. (2006). Improving relationships within the schoolhouse. *Educational Leadership*, *63*(6), 8–13.

Bauch, P. A. (1984, April). *The impact of teachers' beliefs on their teaching: Implications for research and practice.* Paper presented at the annual meeting of the American Educational Research Association, New Orleans, Louisiana.

Borko, H., & Putnam, R. T. (1995). Expanding a teacher's knowledge base: A cognitive psychological perspective on professional development. In T. R. Guskey & M. Huberman (Eds.), *Professional development in education: New paradigms and practices* (pp. 35–65). New York: Teachers College Press.

Bryk, A. S., & Schneider, B. (2002). *Trust in schools. A core resource for improvement.* New York: Sage Foundation.

Buchanan-Rivera, E. (2017, May). *Development of an instrument to assess cultural inclusiveness within a physical classroom environment.* Unpublished dissertation, Indiana State University, Terre Haute, Indiana.

Cairns, J. A. (n.d.). *Why perfection is the enemy of excellence* [Blog post]. Accessed at https:// theabundancecode.com/blog/perfection-enemy-of-excellence on May 19, 2021.

Cialdini, R. (2016). *Pre-suasion: A revolutionary way to influence and persuade.* New York: Simon & Schuster.

Ciardi, M., Gordon, G., Greenburg, R., Greene, J., Mone, J., & O'Connor, G. (Producers), & O'Connor, G. (Director). (2004). *Miracle* [Motion picture]. United States: Walt Disney Pictures.

Creswell, J. W., & Poth, C. N. (2018). *Qualitative inquiry and research design: Choosing among five approaches* (4th ed.). Los Angeles: SAGE.

Deal, T. E., & Kennedy, A. A. (1982). *Corporate cultures: The rites and rituals of corporate life.* Reading, MA: Addison-Wesley.

Deal, T. & Peterson, K. D. (1990). *The principal's role in shaping school culture.* Washington DC: U.S. Government Printing Office.

Deal, T. E., & Peterson, K. D. (1999). *Shaping school culture: The heart of leadership.* San Francisco: Jossey-Bass.

Deal, T. E., & Peterson, K. D. (2016). *Shaping school culture: Pitfalls, paradoxes, and promises* (3rd ed.). San Francisco: Jossey-Bass.

DeAngelis, T. (2015, March). In search of cultural competence. *American Psychological Association, 46*(3), 64. Accessed at apa.org/monitor/2015/03/cultural-competence on May 27, 2021.

Ethnographer. (n.d.). In *Cambridge dictionary online.* Accessed at https://dictionary.cambridge .org/us/dictionary/english/ethnographer on May 6, 2021.

Florio-Ruane, S. (2001). *Teacher education and the cultural imagination: Autobiography, conversation, and narrative.* Mahwah, NJ: Erlbaum.

Forbes. (2015, December). *Drucker said 'culture eats strategy for breakfast' and Enterprise Rent-A-Car proves it.* Accessed at www.forbes.com/sites/shephyken/2015/12/05/drucker-said-culture -eats-strategy-for-breakfast-and-enterprise-rent-a-car-proves-it on June 7, 2021.

Frank, C. (1999). *Ethnographic eyes: A teacher's guide to classroom observation.* Portsmouth, NH: Heinemann.

French, J. R. P., & Raven, B. H. (1959). The bases of social power. In D. Cartwright (Ed.), *Studies in social power* (pp. 150–167). Ann Arbor, MI: Institute for Social Research.

Fullan, M. (1997). *What's worth fighting for in the principalship?* New York: Teachers College Press.

Fullan, M. (2011). *Change leader: Learning to do what matters most.* San Francisco: Jossey-Bass.

Fullan, M., & Hargreaves, A. (1996). *What's worth fighting for in your school?* Buckingham: Open University Press.

Gilmour, D., & Waters, R. (1980). Comfortably numb [Recorded by Pink Floyd]. On *The Wall* [Audio file]. New York: Sony Music Entertainment. Accessed at www.youtube.com /watch?v=_FrOQC-zEog on May 4, 2021.

Gladwell, M. (2013). *David and Goliath: Underdogs, misfits, and the art of battling giants.* New York: Little, Brown.

Glasser, W. (1994). *The control theory manager: Combining the control theory of William Glasser with the wisdom of W. Edwards Deming to explain both what quality is and what lead-managers do to achieve it.* New York: HarperBusiness.

Glasser, W. (1999). *Choice theory: A new psychology of personal freedom.* New York: HarperCollins Publishers.

Godin, S. (2012). *All marketers are liars: The underground classic that explains how marketing really works—and why authenticity is the best marketing of all.* New York: Portfolio.

Grissom, J. A., Egalite, A. J., & Lindsay, C. A. (2021, February). *How principals affect students and schools: A systematic synthesis of two decades of research* [Research report]. New York: Wallace Foundation. Accessed at https://wallacefoundation.org/knowledge-center/Documents/How -Principals-Affect-Students-and-Schools.pdf on March 8, 2021.

Gruenert, S. (2008). *School culture, school climate: They are not the same thing.* Accessed at www
.naesp.org/sites/default/files/resources/2/Principal/2008/M-Ap56.pdf on March 8, 2021.

Gruenert, S., & Valentine, J. (1998). *Development of a school culture survey.* Unpublished
dissertation, University of Missouri, Columbia, Missouri.

Gruenert, S., & Whitaker, T. (2015). *School culture rewired: How to define, assess, and transform it.*
Alexandria, VA: Association for Supervision and Curriculum Development.

Gruenert, S., & Whitaker, T. (2017). *School culture recharged: Strategies to energize your staff and
culture.* Alexandria, VA: Association for Supervision and Curriculum Development.

Gruenert, S., & Whitaker, T. (2019). *Committing to the culture: How leaders can create and sustain
positive schools.* Alexandria, VA: Association for Supervision and Curriculum Development.

Hill, A., Mellon, L., Laker, B., & Goddard, J. (2017). Research: How the best school leaders create
enduring change. *Harvard Business Review.* Accessed at https://hbr.org/2017/09/research
-how-the-best-school-leaders-create-enduring-change on July 7, 2021.

Lewin, K. (1951). *Field theory in social science: Selected theoretical papers.* New York: Harper.

Little, J. W. (1990). The persistence of privacy: Autonomy and initiative in teachers' professional
relations. *Teachers College Record, 91*(4), 509–536.

Lortie, D. C. (1975). *Schoolteacher: A sociological study.* Chicago: University of Chicago Press.

Maslow, A. H. (1943). A theory of human motivation. *Psychological Review, 50*(4), 370–396.

McGregor, D. (1960). *The human side of enterprise.* New York: McGraw-Hill.

Murphy, K. (2020). *You're not listening: What you're missing and why it matters.* New York: Celadon
Books.

National Association of Secondary School Principals. (2021). *NASSP and LPI research agenda:
Understanding and addressing principal turnover research review.* Accessed at www.nassp.org
/nassp-and-lpi-research-agenda on July 7, 2021.

Patterson, K., Grenny, J., Maxfield, D., McMillan, R., & Switzler, A. (2008). *Influencer: The power
to change anything.* New York: McGraw-Hill.

Paul, R., & Elder, L. (2009). Critical thinking: Ethical reasoning and fairminded thinking, part I.
Journal of Developmental Education, 33(1), 38–39.

Reiner, R., Brown, D., & Scheinman, A. (Producers), & Reiner, R. (Director). (1992). *A few good
men* [Motion picture]. United States: Columbia Pictures.

Robbins, H. A., & Finley, M. (2000). *The new why teams don't work: What goes wrong and how to
make it right.* San Francisco: Berrett-Koehler.

Rosenholtz, S. J. (1991). *Teachers' workplace: The social organization of schools.* New York: Teachers
College Press.

Sarason, S. B. (1971). *The culture of the school and the problem of change.* Boston: Allyn & Bacon.

Sarason, S. B. (1996). *Revisiting "the culture of school and the problem of change."* New York:
Teachers College Press.

Schein, E. H. (1985). *Organizational culture and leadership* (1st ed.). San Francisco: Jossey-Bass.

Schein, E. H. (1992). *Organizational culture and leadership: A dynamic view* (3rd ed.). San Francisco: Jossey-Bass.

Schein, E. H. (2009). *Helping: How to offer, give, and receive help*. San Francisco: Berrett-Koehler.

Schein, E. H. (2017). *Organizational culture and leadership* (5th ed.). Hoboken, NJ: Wiley.

Senge, P., Cambron-McCabe, N., Lucas, T., Smith, B., Dutton, J., & Kleiner, A. (2012). *Schools that learn: A fifth discipline fieldbook for educators, parents, and everyone who cares about education*. New York: Crown Business.

Senge, P. M., Kleiner, A., Roberts, C., Rosse, R. B., & Smith, B. J. (2014). *The fifth discipline fieldbook: Strategies and tools for building a learning organization*. New York: Currency.

Sergiovanni, T. J. (2001). *The principalship: A reflective practice perspective* (4th ed.). Boston: Allyn & Bacon.

Shapiro, J. (2000). Consequences of the psychological contract for the employment relationship: A large scale survey. *Journal of Management Studies, 37*(7), 904–930.

Sibony, O. (2020). *You're about to make a terrible mistake: How biases distort decision-making—and what you can do to fight them*. New York: Little, Brown Spark.

Stalbaum, E. (2021). *A continuum of systems thing: From systematic to systemic*. Unpublished dissertation, Indiana State University, Terre Haute, Indiana.

"Subculture." (n.d.) In *Merriam-Webster.com*. Accessed at www.merriam-webster.com/dictionary /subculture on June 3, 2021.

Tsipursky, G. (2020). *What is unconscious bias (and how you can defeat it): Research-based strategies for how to identify and defeat unconscious bias*. Accessed at www.psychologytoday.com/us /blog/intentional-insights/202007/what-is-unconscious-bias-and-how-you-can-defeat-it on July 13, 2021.

Wagner, T. (2000). *How schools change: Lessons from three communities revisited* (2nd ed.). New York: RoutledgeFalmer.

Whitaker, T. (2010). *Leading school change: Nine strategies to bring everybody on board*. Larchmont, NY: Eye on Education.

Whitaker, T. (2020). *What great principals do differently: Twenty things that matter most* (3rd ed.). New York: Routledge.

Woodman, R. W., & Pasmore, W. A. (Eds.). (1996). *Research in organizational change and development* (Vol. 9). Bingley, England: Emerald.

Index

A

activities for school improvement, 131
affective domain, 60
assessments
    computing a mean score for, 92–97
    individual social influence, 91–92
    individual's capacity to change, 90–92
    what's most important at work, 117
    what's most important in life, 115
assimilating opinions, 15, 19
assumptions, 54–55, 77–78, 104
    guiding capacity to change, 88–90
attendance, 43–44, 46–47
attitude, 43, 45–46
    teacher's effects on classroom culture, 53–56
attractive/repelling others
    using culture, 16, 19
autonomy
    independent classroom culture, 58, 60

B

being culture-bound, 8
beliefs, 44, 113
    foundation of a culture, 105
    teachers', 55
belonging, 7–8
bias, 27, 78–79
    confirmatory, 77
Brown, D., 81
building psychological comfort through patterns, 17, 19
building-level norms, 25
burned-out classroom culture, 59–66

C

capacity to change, 9, 87–88
    assessments, 91–92
    assumptions guiding, 88–90
    graphic example, 96
    process for change, 90–97
    speed of culture change, 97–99
caring culture, 12–14, 82
ceremonies. *See* rituals, routines, and ceremonies

changing classroom culture, 73–75
    assessments, 91–92
    assumptions guiding, 88–90
    baseline for, 129–130
    before you begin, 127–130
    necessity of, 9, 107–111
    peer influence, 88–89
    playbook for, 130–132
    process for change, 90–97
    resistance, 87–88
    speed of culture change, 97–99
    student buy-in, 74
choice theory (Glasser), 17
classroom culture, 9, 51–53
    as a reflection of teacher attitude and mindset, 53–56
    assessment, 66–73
    change, 73–75
    typology of, 56–66
    typology wheel, 72
classroom scorecard, 82–85
    comparing and contrasting, 84
climate, 67–68, 113
    as a tool, 47–49
    can improve schools, 1–2, 9–20
    commonalities with culture, 41
    defined, 2
    elements of, 9, 43–50
    impacts of changing on culture, 4–7
    scenarios, 31–33
    theoretical foundations, 7–9
    vs. culture, 2–4, 23–41
collaborative culture, 8, 21, 62–63, 82
    building, 13
    classroom traits, 58
collective capacity to change, 89
commonalities of culture and climate, 41
communication, 67–68
confirmatory bias, 27
The Control Theory Manager (Glasser), 7
convincing members of their normalcy, 18–19
core values, 82
Corporate Cultures (Deal & Kennedy), 1
COVID-19 pandemic, 26
    remote learning, 36–37

"Critical Thinking" (Paul & Elder), 8
cultural competence, 23–24
culture. *See also* classroom culture; school culture
    as an excuse for failure, 6–7
    assessing, 66–76, 101–105
    can improve schools, 1–2, 9–10
    change, 73–75
    classroom scorecard, 82–85
    collaborative, 8
    commonalities with climate, 41
    comparing and contrasting scorecards, 84
    confusion between culture and climate change,
        33–38
    defining, 2, 9, 11–12
    elements of, 43–47
    impacts of changing climate, 4–7
    introductions scorecard, 78–82
    irrational, 20–22
    misalignment, 116
    necessity of change, 9, 107–111
    organizational, 23–26
    personal traits scorecard, 80–81
    right one, 121–125
    scenarios, 28–30, 33–38
    scorecard, 77
    small, 51, 51–75
    theoretical foundations, 7–9
    three levels, 77–78
    traits, 12–14
    typology of, 56–66
    vs. climate, 2–4, 23, 26–33, 38–41
    what culture tries to do, 14–20

D

data analysis, 105
Deal, T. E., 1, 24
defining school culture, 9, 11–12
    culture traits, 12–14
    irrational cultures, 20–22
    what cultures try to do, 14–20
    What Is Your School Culture Doing? form, 19
dependent variables, 101
determining an individual's capacity to
change, 90–92
assessment form, 91
discomfort as a rite of passage, 3–4
diversity of thought
    using culture to minimize, 14–15, 19–20
Drucker, P., 108

E

Elder, L., 8
elements of climate, 9, 49–50
    school climate as a tool, 47–49
    vs. elements of culture, 43–47
Employment Opportunity Act, 79

Equal Employment Opportunity commission, 79
espoused values, 77
ethnographers, 55

F

false realities, 5
A Few Good Men (Reiner et al.), 81
freedom, 7
frozen systems, 39
Fullan, M., 24
fun, 7

G

Glasser, W., 7
glorifying the unknown, 18
Google Maps, 97
Gruenert, S., 56, 96, 113, 129

H

happiness
    culture and, 18
    redefining to fit the norm, 87
helpless classroom cultures, 59, 64–65
heroes, 44, 113
hiding, 18–19
hierarchy of needs (Maslow), 7
hiring new staff, 18, 38–39
humor, 69–70

I

identifying leaders, 16–17, 19
identifying opponents, 16, 19
identifying the right culture, 124–125
identifying whom to trust and listen to, 17, 19
improving test scores, 18
independent classroom culture, 58, 60
independent variables, 101
Indiana State University, ix
individual social influence, 91–92
    assessment form, 92
    matrix example, 93
    matrix with cell weights example, 94
    matrix with scores total per row example, 95
Influencer (Patterson et al.), 96
innovation, 125
interviews, 104
introductions scorecard, 78–82
irrational cultures, 20–22

J

Justice Laws website, 79

K

Kennedy, A. A., 1

L

Ladder of Inference, 27
language, 44, 113
leadership influences capacity to change, 89
Lewin, K., 39
Little, J. W., 24
Lortie, D. C., 24
loyalty, 43, 46

M

Maslow, A., 7
Massachusetts Institute of Technology, 24
meanness, 65
mindset, 78–79
    teacher's effects on classroom culture, 53–56
mission, 43, 113
morale, 43, 45

N

necessity of culture change, 9, 107–108
    unchangeable cultures, 108–110
    warning signs, 9, 110–111
negative culture, 109
norms, 44, 113
    redefining happiness to fit, 87

O

observations, 103
    classrooms, 103
    formal meetings, 104
    hallways, 103
    informal gatherings, 104
    lunch rooms, 103–104
organic classroom culture, 58–59, 63–64
organizational culture, 23–26
    defined, 24
    vs. organizational climate, 26–33
other teachers, 69–70

P

Patterson, K., 96
Paul, R., 8
pedagogy, 67–68
peer influence, 21, 88–89
personal traits scorecard, 80–81
Peterson, K. D., 24
Pink Floyd, 3
playbook for cultural change, 130–132
power, 7
prejudice, 27, 78–79
principal's role, 69–70
problems
    need for, 48

process for change, 90
    before you begin, 127–130
    computing a mean score for each assessment, 92–93
    computing a mean score for the school, 93–97
    determine individual capacity, 90–92
    playbook for cultural change, 130–132

Q

qualitative research approach, 101–102
    data, 105
    interviews, 104
    observations, 103–104
    themes, 102–103

R

"range of normal," 4
Reiner, R., 81
relevance, 74
resistance to change, 4–7
rewarding loyalty
    using cultures, 17, 19
rewires, 113, 129
the right culture, 9, 121–122
    examples, 122–124
    identifying, 124–125
    what it looks like, 122–124
rituals, routines, and ceremonies, 25, 44, 113
Rosenholtz, S. J., 24
rounding up, 80
routines. *See* rituals, routines, and ceremonies
rules, 113
    unwritten, 53–54, 124

S

Sarason, S. B., 24
satisfaction, 43–45
saturation, 102
scenarios
    climate, not culture, 30–32
    confusion between culture and climate change, 33–38
    culture, not climate, 28–30
    difference between culture and climate, 38–40
Schein, E. H., 24, 54–55, 77, 104
Scheinman, A., 81
School Culture Rewired (Gruenert & Whitaker), 56, 96
    School Culture Typology Activity (Gruenert & Whitaker), 56

school culture
    assessment, 101
    culture traits, 12–14
    data analysis, 105
    defining, 9, 11–12
    irrational cultures, 20–22

qualitative research, 101–104
rewires, 113, 129
what cultures try to do, 14–20
What Is Your School Culture Doing? form, 19
scorecards
classroom, 82–84
comparing and contrasting, 84
culture, 77–78
introductions, 78–82
personal traits, 81
self-assessment, 70–71
Shaping School Culture (Deal & Peterson), 24
Shifting the Monkey (Whitaker), ix
Sibony, O., 14–15
small culture. *See* classroom culture; school culture
speed of culture change, 97–99
stories, 44, 113
student chemistry, 67–68
subcultures, 27, 52
survival
basic need, 7
using culture to teach skills, 15–16, 19–20
symbols, 44, 77, 113

T

teacher "locker rooms," 11
teacher mindset
affects classroom culture, 53–56
teacher satisfaction, 27–38
The Ten-Minute Inservice (Whitaker), ix
themes, 102–103
theory of capacity to change
assumptions guiding, 88–90
three levels of culture
assumptions, 77–78
espoused values, 77
symbols, 77
tools, 43
school climate as, 47–49
toxic classroom culture, 59, 65, 79, 110
traditional classroom culture, 57–60
traditions, 25, 67–70
traits, 12–14
tribalism, 20–21
trust, 20–22, 67–68
as a luxury, 66
Tsipursky, G., 78

typology of classroom cultures, 56–57
burned out, 59, 66
collaborative, 58, 62–63
helpless, 59, 64–65
independent, 58, 60
organic, 58–59, 63–64
toxic, 59, 65
traditional, 57–60
warm and fuzzy, 58, 60–62

U

unchangeable cultures, 107–110
University of California, Berkeley, 24
University of Chicago, 24
University of Missouri, ix
unwritten rules, 53–54, 124

V

Valentine, J., ix
value change to culture change, 116–119
values, 9, 44, 113–114
assessment forms, 115, 117
classroom scorecard, 82–84
core, 82
defined, 113
espoused, 77
foundation of a culture, 105
value change to change culture, 116–119
what's most important at work, 116
what's most important in life, 114–116
vision, 43, 113

W

Wagner, T., 82
warm and fuzzy classroom culture, 58, 60–62
warning signs, 9, 110–111
weak school culture, 52, 114–116
What Great Teachers Do Differently (Whitaker), ix
what's most important?
assessment forms, 115, 117
at work, 116
in life, 114–116
Whitaker, T., 26–27, 56, 96, 113, 129

Y

Yale University, 24

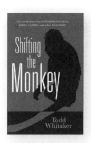

Shifting the Monkey
Todd Whitaker
Learn how to focus on your best employees first, and help them shift the "monkeys"—complaints, disruptions, and deflections—back to the underperformers. Through a simple and memorable metaphor, the author helps you reinvigorate your staff and transform your organization.
BKF612

Transforming School Culture, Second Edition
Anthony Muhammad
The second edition of this best-selling resource delivers powerful, new insight into the four types of educators and how to work with each group to create thriving schools. The book also includes Dr. Muhammad's latest research and a new chapter of frequently asked questions.
BKF793

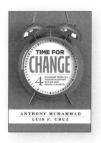

Time for Change
Anthony Muhammad and Luis F. Cruz
Exceptional leaders have four distinctive skills: strong communication, the ability to build trust, the ability to increase the skills of those they lead, and a results orientation. *Time for Change* offers powerful guidance for those seeking to develop and strengthen these skills.
BKF683

Building a Culture of Hope
Robert D. Barr and Emily L. Gibson
Discover a blueprint for turning low-performing schools into cultures of hope. The authors draw from their own experiences working with high-poverty, high-achieving schools to illustrate how to support students with an approach that considers social as well as emotional factors.
BKF503

Solution Tree | Press

a division of
Solution Tree

Visit SolutionTree.com or call 800.733.6786 to order.

Wait! Your professional development journey doesn't have to end with the last pages of this book.

We realize improving student learning doesn't happen overnight. And your school or district shouldn't be left to puzzle out all the details of this process alone.

No matter where you are on the journey, we're committed to helping you get to the next stage.

Take advantage of everything from **custom workshops** to **keynote presentations** and **interactive web and video conferencing**. We can even help you develop an action plan tailored to fit your specific needs.

Let's get the conversation started.

Call 888.763.9045 today.